Lean Star Cuisine

Lean Star Cuisine

From The Kitchen of Lake Austin Spa Resort

By Terry Conlan

Food Services Director

Lake Austin
spa resort

LEAN STAR CUISINE

Cover design by Terry Conlan
Illustrations by Charles Loving

Edited by Trisha Shirey

Third Printing, November 1996

ISBN 0-9619476-1-6

DEDICATION

To M.F.K. Fisher and Michael Fields, who knew.
And to all of the rest of us,
who are still learning.

ACKNOWLEDGEMENTS

No project of this sort is without its share of vital, but unsung, contributors, so allow me to sing a little.

To Trisha Shirey, whose gardens literally provided so much of the material for this book, and who as editor spent countless hours hammering my handwritten scrabble into something the rest of the world might hope to understand, I am inexhaustibly indebted. (A fact I expect to be reminded of occasionally.) Many thanks to Betty Jo Evans for her valuable expertise and tireless efforts at the computer.

A special thanks to Deborah Evans, our director (and the author of <u>Spa Specialties</u>) and to Cindy Present, our marketing manager, both of whom provided continued and much appreciated encouragement and advice.

To Cynthia Maddox, Janis Simms, and Linda Dielman for their support and assistance in promoting this book.

And lastly, to our kitchen staff; that dedicated, indefatigable group of "range rangers" who make it all worthwhile for me, and whose countless contributions continue to bring these recipes to life everyday: Mike Conner, Ruben Reynolds, Audrey Smith, Shirley Mixen, Jose Perez, Pauline Shaw, Simone Shepperd, Vanessa Kahoutek, Connie Vann, Emilio Delgado, Julio Sauceda, Tony Alvarez, and Todd Varnedoe.

Thank you.

INTRODUCTION

At Lake Austin Spa Resort, our philosophies regarding total wellness and good eating evolve as continuously as the river that runs beside us. New ideas, foods, and recipes rise to present themselves, old ones ask to be re-examined or re-worked.

The recipes in the resort's original cookbook, <u>Spa Specialties</u>, served, and continue to serve us well. (Almost half of what we prepare still emanates from this source.) However, we now have many more that we would like to share. This companion cookbook represents a compilation of the best of our new recipes.

The food in this new cookbook is not dietetic. It is not specifically designed to help you lose weight; in fact, it is not about loss at all, but rather about what is to be gained...color, flavor, texture and <u>good nutrition</u> abound. It is about eating "right".

The dual driving considerations behind each and every recipe were not only whether or not the finished dish was good for you, but equally whether or not it was "just plain good"; and no recipe could so satisfy the first half of this equation as to overrule the second. We are fairly passionate about that. The real acid tests for our new recipes were: could they stand on their own merits, was this food that you would <u>want</u> to eat, that you would eagerly <u>choose</u>, mindful and pleased in the knowledge of, but not simply coerced by, the fact that it was "good for you". We think so.

In a very real sense this book is as much yours as ours; your participation, or partnership, in this grand and ongoing experiment, as a guest at Lake Austin Spa Resort, has greatly directed and shaped the book's outcome; your feedback and support on these issues has been instrumental and inspirational, invaluable and gratifying. Enjoy!

Yours for continued great eating,

Terry Conlan

TABLE OF CONTENTS

Appetizers

BRAZOS BEAN DIP

Actually made with split peas rather than beans, but no matter, this spicy spread tastes good and is good for you. You might even slide it past those folks who don't eat "health food" but will try anything on a tortilla chip. We like the blue chips, if you can find them, for color contrast.

2 cups dried yellow split peas
1 quart water or chicken stock
1/2 cup onion, chopped
2 cloves garlic, minced
2 fresh jalapeños, seeded and minced (or other hot green pepper)
1/4 cup water
1/4 cup corn oil
2 teaspoons cumin
1 teaspoon chili powder
1/2 cup cilantro, chopped

Simmer peas in broth approximately 45 minutes until tender, being careful not to scorch. Cool.

Puree onion, garlic, peppers in food processor. Add split peas and remaining ingredients and process again, briefly.

Pipe onto fresh vegetable pieces or serve with baked corn tortilla chips.

Yield: 2 quarts

16 calories / .4 grams fat per tablespoon

CRAB DIP

Simple and oh so sea-easy. Use only fresh lump crab meat, not the canned stuff which has all the taste and texture of shredded cellophane.

2 cups yogurt cheese (see glossary for instructions)
1 cup mock sour cream (page 72)
Juice of one lime
1 tablespoon fresh dill, chopped
2 cloves garlic, minced
1/4 teaspoon cayenne
1/4 teaspoon garlic powder
1/4 teaspoon onion powder
1/2 pint fresh crab meat, picked over to remove shells

Thoroughly combine all ingredients except crab meat. Gently fold in crab meat. Chill.

Serve with crackers or vegetable crudites.

Yield: 1 quart

19 calories / trace of fat per tablespoon

CHICKEN PATE

This picante poultry spread is just hot enough to tempt you to say, "It's my pate and I can cry if I want to." Resist this temptation at all costs.

1 teaspoon vegetable oil
1/2 cup onion, chopped
2 tablespoons fresh jalapeño pepper, seeded and chopped
1 clove garlic, minced
1 pound ground chicken breast
1 teaspoon cumin
1 teaspoon chili powder
1/4 teaspoon salt
1/4 teaspoon freshly ground black pepper
1/4 cup chopped cilantro
1 teaspoon lime zest
1/2 cup nonfat mayonnaise
2 tablespoons lime juice

Gently saute vegetables in oil until tender.

Add chicken and cook, crumbling until done. Drain.

Combine with remaining ingredients in a food processor. Blend until smooth, scraping down sides once. Chill.

Yield: 1 quart

22 calories / .75 grams fat per tablespoon

CURRIED CHICKEN CROUSTADES

This is an excellent way to incorporate leftover meats into tasty appetizers. Turkey, beef, lamb or shrimp would all substitute nicely for the chicken.

1 loaf whole wheat bread
vegetable cooking spray

Spray a 2 ounce-size muffin tin with vegetable spray. Cut circular cookie shapes from bread slices; press firmly into muffin tins and bake at 300 degrees for 20 minutes. (Save the crusts for croutons, bread crumbs or to feed the birds.)

1/2 apple, peeled and diced
2 teaspoons margarine
1/3 onion, minced
1/2 cup celery, minced
1 tablespoon flour
1 1/2 teaspoons curry powder
1/2 cup chicken stock
3/4 pound chicken breast, cooked and diced
1/4 cup mock sour cream (page 72)
1/4 cup light sour cream
1 cup chutney

Saute onion, apple, celery in margarine until softened. Blend in flour and curry powder; cook for one minute.

Whisk in warm chicken stock and cook until slightly thickened. Remove from heat, stir in remaining ingredients and chill.

Fill prepared croustades just before serving and garnish with chutney.

Yield: 24 servings

72 calories / 1.75 grams fat per serving

CURRIED LENTILS

The simplicity and solid texture of the lentils make a nice counterpoint to the hip hop snap of the Eastern spices and hot pepper.

1 tablespoon vegetable oil
1 small onion, minced
6 cloves garlic, minced
1 rib celery, minced
1 tablespoon fresh ginger, peeled and minced
1 tablespoon curry powder
1 teaspoon tumeric
1/4 teaspoon cayenne
2 tomatoes, seeded and diced
1 serrano pepper, seeded and minced
Juice of one lemon
2 cups lentils, rinsed
6 cups water

Saute onion, garlic, celery, and ginger in oil until softened; add spices, cook 1 minute; add tomatoes, cook 1 minute; add water and lentils, bring to a boil, reduce to simmer. Cook 30 to 45 minutes until lentils are soft and liquid has evaporated. You may add liquid if needed.

Stir in lemon juice and serrano pepper. Chill.

Serve with crackers or in croustades. (See the Curried Chicken Croustade recipe on the previous page.)

Yield: 1 quart

16 calories/ .2 grams fat per tablespoon

EGGPLANT SPREAD

Baking the garlic mellows the flavor and gives it a rich, creamy texture. Cook an extra head of garlic and try some spread simply over a piece of toasted French bread.

2 whole heads of garlic
1 large eggplant, pricked several times with a fork
Juice from 1/2 lemon
1 tablespoon olive oil
Pinch of cayenne
Pinch of salt
Olive oil flavored vegetable cooking spray

Remove the papery outer shell from the garlic heads, leaving whole. Spray with cooking spray, wrap each head individually in foil.

Bake garlic and eggplant at 400 degrees about 45 minutes. Cool.

Cut the eggplant in half and scoop out the pulp.

Use scissors to clip the tops off the garlic heads, squeeze the garlic paste from the papery shells and combine with the eggplant, lemon juice, oil, seasonings.

Serve at room temperature with crackers or toasted French bread slices.

Yield: 4 cups

12 calories /.25 grams fat per tablespoon

GARLIC BREAD WITH FRESH TOMATOES AND BASIL

Don't be misled by the simplicity of this recipe. If you hold in hand a garden ripe tomato, fresh basil, garlic, good bread and olive oil, you hold history, health, and a hint of what heaven might have to offer.

6 slices day-old sourdough French bread, sliced diagonally
1 ripe tomato, diced
4 leaves fresh basil
1 teaspoon extra virgin olive oil
2 large garlic cloves, cut in half
Freshly ground black pepper

Shred the basil with your hands and gently mix with the tomatoes and olive oil. Allow to stand for several hours.

Toast bread slices at 400 degrees on both sides. (The bread may also be toasted on the grill.)

Rub the crusts of the bread with the cut side of the garlic cloves.

Top each bread slice with the tomato mixture and serve immediately.

Yield: 6 servings

32 calories / .8 grams fat per serving

Contributed by Trisha Shirey

PESTO DIP

Traditionally, pesto is made with lots of olive oil, but in this version, Trisha has substituted yogurt cheese to create a delicious dip with a fraction of the fat. Try some the next time you want to go "skinny dipping".

2 cloves garlic, or more to taste
1 cup fresh basil leaves, stems removed and loosely packed
1/4 cup Italian parsley, stems removed and loosely packed
2 tablespoons pine nuts
2 tablespoons freshly grated Parmesan cheese
1 cup nonfat yogurt cheese (see Glossary)

Drop garlic into the small feeder chute of a food processor while the motor is running. Remove the processor cover and add the basil, parsley, pine nuts and Parmesan cheese. Use the pulse button to blend to a smooth paste. Stop and stir with a spatula as needed.

Add the yogurt cheese and process for a few seconds to mix. Don't over process the yogurt cheese or it will become runny.

Chill for 2 hours before serving. Serve with crackers or as a vegetable dip or use as a pasta salad dressing.

Yield: 1 1/4 cups

17 calories/ .5 grams fat per tablespoon

This recipe may also be made with fresh dill or with lemon basil. Substitute sliced almonds for the pine nuts for a more delicate flavor.

Contributed by Trisha Shirey

PUMPKIN SEED DIP

For a full appreciation of the fresh roasted, nutty flavor of this dip, try to make it just a couple of hours before you plan to serve it. You can char the tomatoes using tongs over a gas burner and the whole process will take less than ten minutes. (Which is about how long it will last when it hits the table.)

Pumpkin seeds are also commonly known as "pepitas" and are available in most health food stores as well as some of the major chains.

2 1/2 cups pumpkin seeds
1 hot green chile, grilled and seeded (serrano, jalapeño)
3 tomatoes, charred over open flame or in a broiler
1 1/2 teaspoons salt
4 tablespoons chopped cilantro
4 tablespoons minced chives

Toast pumpkin seeds well by tossing in a dry skillet over medium heat. Puree seeds in a food processor.

Add remaining ingredients and blend briefly. Serve chilled or at room temperature with baked tortilla chips.

Yield: 4 cups

11 calories / .9 grams fat per teaspoon serving

SHRIMP QUESADILLAS

These slightly sweet, slightly spicy, delectable little turnovers may be kept unbaked under a damp towel for a while, but once baked, should be served as soon as possible. If you are making a lot of them for a party, you will probably need someone who is the equivalent of the "designated driver" to keep them coming.

Filling:
4 ounces low fat cheddar
1 pound shrimp, peeled and chopped
2 cloves garlic, minced
1/2 onion, minced
2 tablespoons minced chives
1 tablespoon adobo paste from canned chipotle peppers
1 tablespoon sugar
2 tablespoons minced cilantro
1 teaspoon orange juice concentrate
1 teaspoon olive oil
Vegetable cooking spray

Saute onion and garlic in oil and vegetable spray until slightly softened. Add the shrimp and cook until just done. Cool.

Combine with all other ingredients. Use to fill the quesadillas.

Dough:
4 cups Masa Harina flour (available in the flour section of most grocery stores)

Combine the masa flour with just enough water to make a soft pliable dough. Knead for a couple of minutes. Divide into walnut sized balls. Flatten a ball between two plastic freezer bags, using a tortilla press or a rolling pin. Peel off top bag, place some filling just off center, fold bottom bag over to fold masa in half over filling. Gently peel back bag, pinch the open edge of the quesadilla closed, and peel it from the plastic.

Just before serving, bake quesadillas on a sprayed griddle or non-stick pan over medium heat, turning occasionally until dough is slightly crisp. Serve with the salsa of your choice. (See our Sauces section.)

Yield: 24 quesadillas
65 calories / 1.5 grams fat each

SHRIMP "MEATBALLS" WITH TOMATO SAUCE

Another unusual appetizer inspired by the cooking of coastal Mexico. This one is definitely party fare, but don't be put off by the instructions. It's not a hard as it looks. A little more broth, a little less shrimp makes a nice soup.

The sauce:
2 pounds tomatoes, charred on the grill or under a broiler
2 tablespoons vegetable oil
1 onion, minced
6 cloves garlic, minced
2 cups water
2 cups tomato juice
1/4 cup cilantro, chopped

Puree the tomatoes in a food processor. Saute tomatoes, onion, garlic in oil until most of the liquid has evaporated. Add water, tomato juice and cilantro, simmer to a thick soup consistency.

The meatballs:
1 chile ancho, seeded and soaked in warm water
1/2 teaspoon coriander
1/2 teaspoon black pepper
1/2 teaspoon cinnamon
1 teaspoon salt
3 cloves garlic
6 tablespoons water
1 tablespoon vegetable oil
3 pounds small shrimp, peeled, then partially frozen

Puree ancho, seasonings and garlic in blender with the water.

Saute this paste in oil for a couple of minutes.

Blend shrimp in food processor until fairly smooth; mix in the chile paste.

Oil hands lightly to minimize sticking and make small, 1" diameter meat balls. Simmer in covered broth for 15 minutes, turning occasionally. Serve hot.

Yield: 60 "meatballs" (This recipe may be successfully halved for fewer servings.)

24 calories / .8 grams fat per meatball

SMOKED DUCK DUMPLINGS WITH DIPPING SAUCE

Better than a Beijing barbecue and "dim sum".

1 clove garlic, minced
1 teaspoon peeled, minced fresh ginger
1 smoked duck breast, minced (skin removed)
1 red bell pepper, broiled or grilled, peeled and diced
1/2 onion, thickly sliced, broiled or grilled and diced
2 tablespoons cilantro, minced
1 package won ton wrappers
1 quart chicken stock

Combine the first six ingredients and use to stuff the won tons according to package directions.

Cook the dumplings in simmering chicken stock according to package directions, drain, cover with plastic wrap and chill. Serve with dipping sauce.

Dipping Sauce:
2 green onions, minced
2 tcaspoons fresh ginger, minced
1 cup light soy sauce
1 teaspoon sugar
1/2 cup white wine
1 tablespoon sesame oil

Yield: 12 servings

36 calories / 1.5 grams fat per serving

SPINACH PESTO PIE

This silky, savory pie is so rich and deeply flavored that a little goes a long way. A glass of reserve chianti, if you're of a mind, makes a perfect foil. Follow with a rosemary accented roast chicken and spring vegetables. Amaretto coffee. An orange sorbet. A bit of chocolate. La dolce vita, no?

2 1/2 cups low fat cottage cheese, liquid pressed out
10 ounces frozen spinach, thawed and chopped, liquid pressed out
8 ounces low fat cream cheese, cubed
1/4 cup Parmesan cheese
1 egg
2 egg whites
2 cloves garlic, minced
2 teaspoons dried basil
1/4 teaspoon salt
1/8 teaspoon black pepper
Vegetable cooking spray

Preheat oven to 325 degrees. Spray a 9" springform pan with vegetable spray.

Process all ingredients in a food processor until smooth. Pour into pan, bake about 1 hour until firm. Cool slightly before slicing.

Yield: 16 servings

73 calories / 3 grams fat per serving

STUFFED PEAR APPETIZER

These make an interesting, slightly exotic, addition to an hors d'oeuvre tray or a good beginning for something curried and/or Caribbean.

3 pears
5 teaspoons lime juice and zest from one lime
1/4 teaspoon cayenne
1 clove minced garlic
1 teaspoon soy sauce
2 tablespoons brown sugar
1/3 cup dry roasted peanuts, ground

Quarter pears, hollowing out the centers. If not serving immediately, dip each piece into water with a little lemon juice to prevent discoloration.

Combine remaining ingredients and stuff into pear hollows.

Yield: 12 servings

48 calories / 2 grams fat per serving

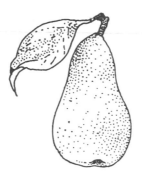

STUFFED ZUCCHINI BOATS

Easy. Inexpensive. A good appetizer to make for large groups. Be sure to get small, bright green zucchini.

1 ten-ounce potato, baked, cooled, peeled and mashed
5 medium zucchini
1 1/2 teaspoons olive oil
1 1/2 teaspoons fresh basil, minced
1 1/2 teaspoons fresh oregano, minced
3 cloves garlic, minced
1/4 cup dry white wine
1/4 cup Parmesan cheese
1/4 cup + 2 tablespoons skim milk
1 tablespoon tomato paste
1/2 teaspoon salt
Vegetable cooking spray

Split the zucchini lengthwise, then crosswise to get four 3-inch lengths from each. Hollow out the "boats"; and reserve 1 cup of pulp. Finely chop the reserved pulp.

Steam the zucchini boats to soften slightly. Invert and drain.

Saute the zucchini pulp, herbs and garlic in oil for 3 minutes. Add wine, and cook until absorbed.

Remove from heat, combine with potato, 3 tablespoons of the cheese, milk, tomato paste, cayenne and salt. Pipe the mixture through a star tipped pastry bag into the boats.

Place on a sprayed baking sheet, sprinkle with the remaining cheese, and bake at 400 degrees for 25 minutes.

Yield: 20 servings

15 calories/ .5 grams fat per serving

TEXAS CAVIAR

You may make this dish successfully with dried black-eyed peas, but fresh peas in season are what the bragging in the title is all about.

1 pound fresh black-eyed peas, cooked and drained.

While the peas are still warm, mix with the following vinaigrette:
2 tablespoons olive oil
2/3 cup lime juice
1 tablespoon Dijon mustard
2 tablespoons herbal vinegar (cilantro)
1 teaspoon oregano

Cool, then add:
1 tomato, diced
2 cups diced red onion
1 cup green onion, minced
1/4 cup jalapeño, minced
1/2 cup red bell pepper, diced
3 cloves garlic, minced
1 tablespoon picante sauce
2 tablespoons cilantro, chopped

Chill. Serve in a bowl garnished with lettuce leaves and top bed with tomato wedges. Accompany with whole wheat crackers or baked tortilla chips. This may also be served as a relish.

Yield: 2 quarts

22 calories / .5 grams fat per serving

WALNUT STUFFED NEW POTATOES

Use the smallest new potatoes you can find and cut a tiny sliver off the bottom of each one so that they will sit upright. I'm sure these clever little casings would also be great stuffed with a variety of leftovers.

24 baby new potatoes, cooked, and hollowed out
24 toasted walnut halves
1 cup light or mock sour cream (page 72)
1 tablespoon minced fresh dill
24 fresh dill sprigs

Steam the potatoes, then hollow out the centers, using an apple parer. Stuff a walnut half into each cavity. Combine minced dill and sour cream and ladle a little into each potato. Top each with a sprig of dill and chill before serving.

Yield: 24 servings

50 calories / 1.7 grams fat per serving

FAT FREE TORTILLA CHIPS

If you are as addicted to chips and hot sauce as you ought to be, it might be a little unsettling to learn that, while corn tortillas themselves are fat free, each commercially fried chip may harbor up to a gram of the stuff. Locally this is known as "being between a rock and a hard place".

Working on the theory that if you can't live with out 'em, you darn sure better learn to live (in this case live longer) with 'em, the way to extricate yourself from this position is to stop buyin' 'em and start bakin' 'em. Just take 10 thin corn tortillas, quarter them with kitchen shears or a sharp knife, spread on a baking sheet and bake in a 350 degree oven until crisp (about 10 minutes).

You may also spray the chips with vegetable cooking spray before baking and sprinkle them with spices. Try chili powder, cumin, onion and garlic powder, or spray with lime juice and chili powder or cayenne. Or add a dab of mashed pinto or black beans, a sprinkle of low fat cheddar and a jalapeño slice - nachos.

Yield: 40 chips

Approximately 15 calories / 0 grams fat per chip

Fat free bagel chips and pita chips may be made in the same way. Freeze the bagel first and thaw slightly, then slice with the slicing attachment of your food processor.

Separate the pita halves and cut into quarters. Sprinkle the pitas or bagels with your choice of dill seed, dill weed, pepper, paprika or garlic powder.

Bread and Breakfast

Few things so entice the senses as the aroma of homemade muffins baking in the oven. At Lake Austin Spa Resort, we bake them every morning. Here's a baker's dozen of our favorites.

APPLE CINNAMON MUFFINS

1 1/4 cups flour
1 1/2 teaspoons baking powder
1 teaspoon cinnamon
1/2 teaspoon clove
1/2 teaspoon baking soda
Pinch of salt
1 ounce brown sugar

Combine the above dry ingredients.

1 cup applesauce
1 egg, slightly beaten
1/2 cup low fat milk
1 tablespoon vegetable oil
1/3 cup raisins
3 tablespoons almonds (or other nut), minced
Vegetable cooking spray

1 tablespoon sugar and 1/2 teaspoon cinnamon to sprinkle on top

Combine wet ingredients in a bowl. Add the dry ingredients and mix together until just moistened. Spray a dozen muffin cups with vegetable spray and divide the batter evenly among the cups. Top each with a little of the cinnamon-sugar mix and bake at 400 degrees for 15 to 20 minutes.

Yield: One dozen

128 calories / 2.5 grams fat per muffin

BANANA RASPBERRY MUFFINS

1 1/4 cups rolled oats
1 cup whole wheat flour
2 tablespoons brown sugar
2 teaspoons baking powder
1/2 teaspoon soda
A pinch of salt
1/2 cup skim milk
2 large egg whites
1 tablespoon vegetable oil
1 cup mashed ripe banana
2 tablespoons sugar free raspberry fruit preserves
Vegetable cooking spray

Combine the first six ingredients. Lightly beat the egg whites and combine with the milk and oil, then add to the dry ingredients along with the banana and stir until just moistened.

Spray muffin tins with the vegetable spray and fill two thirds full with batter.

Place 1/2 teaspoon of the preserves on the center of each muffin.

Bake at 375 degrees for 25 minutes.

Yield: 12 muffins

127 calories / 2 grams fat per muffin

BUTTERMILK BRAN BLUEBERRY MUFFINS

3 cups bran
2 cups whole wheat flour
1/2 cup sugar
1 tablespoon baking powder
1 teaspoon baking soda
2 eggs, beaten
2 cups buttermilk
1/3 cup vegetable oil
1/2 cup molasses
1 cup fresh or frozen blueberries
Vegetable cooking spray

Combine dry ingredients. Combine wet ingredients separately. Fold together.

Fold in the blueberries.

Spray muffin cups with vegetable spray and divide mixture evenly.

Bake at 400 degrees for fifteen minutes

Yield: 20 large muffins

160 calories / 5 grams fat per muffin

CORNMEAL RAISIN SCONES

1 1/2 cups all-purpose flour
1/2 cup stone ground cornmeal
2 tablespoons sugar
1 teaspoon baking powder
1 teaspoon baking soda
1/4 teaspoon salt
2 tablespoons margarine, cut into bits and chilled
1/4 cup golden raisins
3/4 cup buttermilk
Vegetable cooking spray

Combine first six ingredients. Cut in margarine with a pastry blender until mixture resembles coarse meal.

Add raisins. Add buttermilk and mix until just moistened.

Turn out onto a lightly floured surface; knead five times. Roll into an 8" circle; cut into ten wedges. Arrange wedges in a circle 1/4" apart on a sprayed baking sheet.

Bake at 375 degrees for 22 minutes.

Yield: 10 servings

139 calories / 2.7 grams fat per serving

CRANBERRY ORANGE MUFFINS

3/4 cup bran
1 cup whole wheat flour
1/2 cup sugar
1 1/2 teaspoons cinnamon
1 teaspoon baking powder
1 teaspoon baking soda
1 cup whole cranberry sauce
1 egg
1/2 cup buttermilk or yogurt
1/4 cup vegetable oil
1 teaspoon orange rind, grated
Vegetable cooking spray

Combine dry ingredients. Combine wet ingredients separately. Fold together.

Spray muffin cups with vegetable spray and divide out mixture. Bake at 400 degrees for 25 minutes.

Yield: 12 muffins

156 calories / 5 grams fat per muffin

FRUITED BUCKWHEAT MUFFINS

1 cup all-purpose flour
1 cup Granny Smith apples, finely chopped
3/4 cup buckwheat flour
1/3 cup sugar
1/4 cup chopped pitted dates
1 1/2 teaspoons baking powder
1/4 teaspoon baking soda
1/8 teaspoon salt
3/4 cup buttermilk
2 tablespoons vegetable oil
1 egg, lightly beaten
No-stick spray

Combine dry ingredients. Combine wet ingredients separately. Combine the two until just moistened.

Divide into sprayed muffin cups. Bake at 375 degrees for 20 minutes.

Yield: 12 muffins

126 calories / 3.3 grams fat per muffin

MAPLE AND WALNUT SQUASH MUFFINS

1 3/4 cups flour
1 teaspoon baking powder
1/2 teaspoon baking soda
1/8 teaspoon salt
1 teaspoon cinnamon
1/4 cup toasted walnuts, finely chopped
3/4 cup butternut squash, cooked and mashed
2/3 cup nonfat yogurt
1/2 cup maple syrup
2 tablespoons vegetable oil
2 egg whites, lightly beaten
Vegetable cooking spray

Combine first six ingredients.

Combine remaining ingredients separately. Mix together until just moistened.

Divide into sprayed muffin cups. Bake at 400 degrees for 20 minutes.

Yield: 12 muffins

148 calories / 4.2 grams fat per muffin

LEMONY PRUNE MUFFINS

1 1/2 cups all-purpose flour
1/2 cup whole wheat flour
1/3 cup brown sugar, packed
1 teaspoon baking powder
1 teaspoon baking soda
1/4 teaspoon salt
3/4 cup nonfat yogurt
1/2 cup pitted prunes, chopped
2 tablespoons margarine, melted
2 tablespoons lemon juice
1 tablespoon lemon rind, grated
1 egg
Vegetable cooking spray

Combine first six ingredients. Combine remaining ingredients separately.

Mix together until just moistened.

Divide into sprayed muffin cups. Bake at 400 degrees for 15 minutes.

Yield: 12 muffins

146 calories / 2.8 grams fat per muffin

OAT BRAN BANANA RAISIN MUFFINS

1 egg, lightly beaten
1/4 cup vegetable oil
1 cup bananas, mashed
1 teaspoon vanilla
1/2 cup sugar
1 cup whole wheat flour
1 teaspoon baking powder
1 teaspoon baking soda
3/4 cup oat bran
1/2 cup raisins
Vegetable cooking spray

Combine wet ingredients; fold in raisins. Combine dry ingredients separately; fold in bananas. Mix together until just moistened.

Divide into sprayed muffin cups. Bake at 400 degrees for 25 minutes.

Yield: 12 muffins

165 calories / 5 grams fat per muffin

OATMEAL CARROT MUFFINS

1 cup buttermilk
1 cup quick cooking rolled oats
1/2 cup carrots, grated
1/4 cup packed brown sugar
1/4 cup margarine, melted
1 egg, beaten
1 teaspoon grated orange zest
1 cup flour
1 tablespoon baking powder
1/2 teaspoon baking soda
1 teaspoon salt
3/4 cup raisins
1/4 cup granulated sugar
Vegetable cooking spray

Pour buttermilk over oats and let stand overnight.

Mix carrots, brown sugar, margarine, egg and orange zest. Stir into oat
mix.

Sift flour, granulated sugar, baking powder, baking soda and salt together;
fold, along with raisins into batter.

Divide into sprayed muffin cups. Bake at 400 degrees for 25 minutes.

Yield: 12 muffins

176 calories / 5 grams fat per muffin

OATMEAL RAISIN BRAN MUFFINS

1 cup rolled oats (not instant or quick)
3/4 cup whole wheat flour
1/4 cup wheat bran
1/4 cup raisins
1 teaspoon baking soda
2 teaspoons cinnamon
1 1/3 cups buttermilk
1 tablespoon vegetable oil
3 tablespoons honey
1 teaspoon vanilla
Vegetable cooking spray

Mix all dry ingredients together. In another bowl, mix liquid ingredients together.

Combine the wet and dry ingredients and mix gently until just moistened. The batter will be lumpy.

Spray muffin tins with the vegetable spray. Fill two thirds full with batter and bake at 325 degrees for 20 to 25 minutes.

Yield: 12 muffins

110 calories / 2 grams fat per muffin

SWEET POTATO MUFFINS

2 eggs
2 cups peeled, cooked and mashed sweet potatoes
2 tablespoons margarine, softened
1 teaspoon vanilla
3/4 cup corn flour
2/3 cup unbleached flour
1/2 cup sugar
2 tablespoons baking powder
1 teaspoon baking soda
1/2 teaspoon salt
3/4 teaspoon nutmeg
1 1/2 teaspoons cinnamon
1/2 cup raisins
1/4 cup pecans, chopped
2/3 cup buttermilk
Vegetable cooking spray

Whip the sweet potatoes with eggs and margarine until light and fluffy.

Mix dry ingredients together and incorporate into batter alternately with buttermilk.

Divide into sprayed muffin cups. Bake at 400 degrees for 20 minutes.

Yield: 12 muffins

140 calories / 2.8 grams fat per muffin

BLUE CORNMEAL FRITTERS WITH CHILE HONEY

Blue cornmeal is made from a hardy, drought tolerant varietal blue corn grown primarily in New Mexico. It is available at health food stores. You may make this recipe with yellow corn meal, of course, but it will not take you back to Taos.

1 cup blue cornmeal
1 cup whole wheat flour
2 teaspoons baking powder
1 teaspoon baking soda
1 cup frozen corn, thawed and drained
2 green onions, minced
1 teaspoon basil
1 tablespoon apple juice concentrate
2/3 cup evaporated skim milk
2/3 cup nonfat milk
2 egg whites, beaten stiff
Vegetable cooking spray

Mix the first ten ingredients in bowl until just combined.

Gently fold in the egg whites. Do not beat.

Cook on a griddle like pancakes approximately 3 minutes per side. Use vegetable cooking spray as needed to prevent sticking.

Yield: Approximately 20 fritters
59 calories / .28 grams fat per fritter

CHILE HONEY

1 cup honey
1 tablespoon New Mexican chile powder
Juice of one lime

Combine all ingredients and serve with the fritters.
20 calories / 0 grams fat per teaspoon

BLUEBERRY BLUE CORN FRITTERS

These fritters will not make you "blue" at all, in fact, the opposite is true. Try them with chopped pecans and the Chile Honey on page 50.

1/2 cup flour
1/2 cup blue cornmeal
2 tablespoons sugar
1 teaspoon baking powder
1/2 teaspoon baking soda
1/2 teaspoon cinnamon
1 cup nonfat yogurt
3 tablespoons skim milk
1 egg, lightly beaten
1 cup blueberries
Vegetable cooking spray

Combine dry ingredients. Combine wet ingredients separately.

Mix together until just moistened. Fold in blueberries.

Spray a skillet with vegetable cooking spray and cook large spoonfuls of batter over medium heat, turning once.

Yield: 10 fritters

70 calories / .25 grams fat per fritter

GINGERBREAD PANCAKES

Gingerbread pancakes are not so much a recipe as a national inheritance, an heirloom nestled in that part of our collective consciousness that Norman Rockwell knew so well and captured so faithfully. Their mere mention conjures up, in most of us, a multitude of half-imagined memories - cozy farmhouse kitchens where gingham clad grannies pour milk from crockery pitchers and ladle warm feathery flapjacks to sleepy headed kids in flannel pajamas dragging Raggedy Anns and wooden trains into a warm and welcome, awakening world where the only question of the hour is...applesauce or apple butter?

These pancakes are a Sunday morning tradition at Lake Austin Spa Resort; we invite you to join us in keeping the candle lit.

1 cup all-purpose flour
1 1/2 teaspoons baking powder
1/2 teaspoon ground cinnamon
1/2 teaspoon ground ginger
Pinch of ground cloves
1/2 cup skim milk
3 tablespoons molasses
1 tablespoon vegetable oil
1 egg, lightly beaten
Vegetable cooking spray

Combine dry ingredients. Combine wet ingredients separately.

Mix together until just moistened.

Spray a skillet with cooking spray and cook large spoonfuls of batter over medium heat, turning once.

Yield: 8 pancakes

91 calories / 2.2 grams fat per pancake

GINGER PEACH PANCAKES

A great East meets South combination. A couple of these for breakfast will have you feeling "ginger peachy" in nothing flat.

1 cup low fat milk
1 tablespoon lemon juice
1 teaspoon lemon zest
1 cup whole wheat pastry flour
1/4 teaspoon salt
1 teaspoon baking soda
2 teaspoons ground ginger
1/4 teaspoon nutmeg
1/8 teaspoon ground cloves
2 teaspoons vegetable oil
1 tablespoon honey
1 egg, separated
1 medium peach, peeled and chopped
Vegetable cooking spray

Combine milk and lemon juice; allow to curdle.

Sift flour, salt, baking soda and spices.

In a separate bowl, whisk together lemon zest, oil, honey and egg yolk. Whisk in curdled milk.

Beat egg white until stiff, but not dry.

Combine wet and dry ingredients. Fold in egg whites. Fold in peach pieces and ladle dollops of batter onto a hot griddle seasoned with cooking spray.

Yield: 12 pancakes

84 calories / 2 grams fat per pancake

CREPES

I like to think of these as what the French had to use because they didn't have tortillas. Actually, they serve the same purpose: comestible containers for a vast variety of victuals, usually leftovers.

1 large egg
2/3 cup skim milk
1/2 cup flour

Combine all ingredients. Blend until batter is smooth.

Using a non stick skillet, ladle in two tablespoons of batter, tilting the skillet around to distribute. Cook over medium heat for about one minute, until the surface appears dry and the edges are slightly browned.

Pry up one edge and carefully flip the crepe over; cook for an additional twenty seconds, then slide onto a plate. Repeat with remaining batter.

Yield: 12 crepes
46 calories / .9 grams fat per crepe

Fill these with any combination of leftover meats or vegetables, roll up like enchiladas, top with a low fat cream sauce or grated cheese and bake in a hot oven (425 degrees) until bubbly.

The following recipes (found elsewhere in this book) are good examples of potential crepe fillers and sauces to top them with:

Stuffed pork tenderloin with blackberry sauce, page 176
Apple glazed chicken with Horseradish Cream Sauce page 184
Mushroom ravioli filling, with basil cream sauce, page 171
Salmon croquettes, page 219

There are lots of others, of course. All you need is an active, frugal imagination and an average family refrigerator. Later in this book you will find our version of a cross cultural exchange - corn masa crepes - another step towards a global gastronomy.

BREAKFAST AND DESSERT CREPES

This is where I think crepes really come into their own and are the most fun. Here are two fillings we use that, with slight modifications, are suitable for either breakfast or dessert. Fold them into squares and you have Blintzes!

LEMON PINEAPPLE FILLING

1 tablespoon lemon zest, grated
Juice of 1/2 lemon
1/2 cup crushed pineapple
2 cups cottage cheese, drained

Combine all ingredients in a food processor or blender and process briefly.

Place one tablespoon of filling in the middle of a crepe and fold tightly.

15 calories / .15 grams fat per serving

STRAWBERRY APRICOT FILLING

1 teaspoon lemon zest, grated
2 tablespoons natural apricot preserves
1 1/2 cups lowfat cottage cheese, drained
1 cup sliced, fresh strawberries

Blend all ingredients except strawberries briefly in a food processor. Fold in strawberries.

17 calories / .12 gram fat per tablespoon

Top either recipe with powdered sugar if desired.

SKILLET CORNBREAD

An old family recipe with the fat somewhat reduced; you can make it in a regular baking pan instead of a cast iron skillet, but the cast iron gives a crustier bottom and makes a nice presentation.

1 cup buttermilk
1 egg
2 tablespoons margarine, melted
1 1/4 cups cornmeal
1/2 cup flour
1/2 teaspoon salt
1 teaspoon baking powder
1/2 teaspoon baking soda
Vegetable cooking spray

Beat egg and margarine into buttermilk. Mix in cornmeal. Mix in remaining ingredients.

Preheat the oven to 425 degrees; place skillet in oven to heat. Spray skillet thoroughly, fill with batter, bake for 25 minutes. Serve in the skillet.

Yield: 16 servings

68 calories / 2.1 grams fat per serving

Sauces and Salsas

BASIL CREAM SAUCE

Do these two things: one, serve this sauce to company, especially "skinny cooking" skeptics; two, don't bother to tell them that it comes in at less than 20 calories and 1 gram of fat per tablespoon. They won't be impressed; they simply won't believe you.

We like it over homemade ravioli stuffed with wild mushrooms, page 171. You may substitute almonds for the pine nuts but <u>fresh</u> basil only, please.

1/2 cup fresh basil, packed
1 tablespoon extra virgin olive oil
2 teaspoons pine nuts, lightly toasted
1 clove garlic, chopped

Puree basil, pine nuts and garlic in blender while drizzling in olive oil. Combine with:

3/4 cup evaporated skim milk
1 tablespoon nonfat milk powder
1/4 cup Parmesan cheese
1/8 teaspoon cayenne

Heat thoroughly. Do not boil.

Yield: Approximately 2 cups

60 calories / 3 grams fat per 1/4 cup serving

CAJUN DEMIGLACE

Cut the cayenne by half if you fall into the culinary category of "ruffled" rather than "ragin cajun". We serve it, full blast, under the Crawfish in Phyllo Pastry on page 215 .

1/4 cup vegetable oil
1/3 cup flour
1/2 cup minced onion
1/4 cup minced green bell pepper
1/4 cup minced celery
1/4 cup minced carrot
1 clove garlic, minced
1 large bay leaf
1 teaspoon garlic powder
1/2 teaspoon white pepper
1/2 teaspoon thyme
1/4 teaspoon oregano
1/4 teaspoon cayenne pepper
1/4 teaspoon black pepper
1 1/2 cups seafood stock or clam juice
1 1/2 cups strong beef stock
3 tablespoons tomato puree
1 tablespoon worcestershire sauce
2 tablespoons chopped parsley
1/4 cup diced fresh tomato
1/4 cup red wine
2 tablespoons cornstarch
Juice of one lemon

Combine flour and oil in a heavy skillet over medium heat, stirring constantly until you have a medium brown roux. Stir in the vegetables and seasonings, cook one minute.

Combine the stocks and bring to a boil in a large pan. Whisk in roux mixture, add tomato puree and worcestershire.

Simmer for 30 minutes, skimming occasionally. Add parsley and tomato and simmer for 10 minutes.

Combine wine and cornstarch and whisk into the sauce until sauce is slightly thickened. Add the lemon juice.

Yield: Approximately 5 cups

42 calories/ 2.5 grams fat per 1/4 cup serving

MICHAEL CONNER'S "BLACK MAGIC" BARBECUE SAUCE

Mike is one of the chefs at Lake Austin Spa Resort and if he never invented another recipe (unlikely), his reputation would rest secure on the merits of this sweet, dark, smoky barbecue beauty.

1/2 small onion, finely diced
1 clove garlic, minced
1 tablespoon vegetable oil
1/4 cup brown sugar
2 tablespoons blackstrap molasses
1/2 cup creole mustard
2 tablespoons worcestershire sauce
2 ounces dark beer
10 ounces catsup
1 teaspoon tabasco sauce
1/2 teaspoon cayenne
1 tablespoon liquid smoke
1/2 cup cider vinegar

Caramelize onion over high heat with vegetable oil.

Add garlic and brown sugar and reduce heat, stirring until sugar melts and darkens.

Add all other ingredients and simmer, stirring occasionally, over low heat for 30 minutes. Serve as an accompaniment for smoked meats.

Yield: 1 quart

11 calories/ .25 grams fat per tablespoon

SWEET AND SOUR SAUCE FOR FISH

Try this tri-colored Orientally oriented topping just once; we guarantee you will want some "Mao Tsung".

1/4 cup rice vinegar
1 1/2 tablespoons apple juice concentrate
1 1/2 teaspoons soy sauce
1 teaspoon ginger
1 10-ounce can chunk pineapple packed in juice
1/2 green bell pepper, sliced thinly
1/2 red bell pepper, sliced thinly
1/2 onion, chopped
1 tablespoon sherry
1/2 teaspoon cornstarch

Simmer the first five ingredients for 10 minutes. Add peppers and onion. Simmer three minutes. Mix sherry and cornstarch together, then stir into sauce. Simmer for three minutes. Serve over grilled fish.

Yield: Approximately 3 cups

7.5 calories/ trace of fat per tablespoon

CHIPOTLE MAYONNAISE

Chipotles are smoked jalapeños, available dried, or more commonly, canned in adobo paste. We sometimes add a dried one to a pot of beans or use the paste from the canned version to flavor marinades and sauces. A word of caution: these little hummers are HOT! so use sparingly, gradually adjusting upwards to your own personal pain/pleasure level. Removing the seeds will cut down on the fire. Try this mayonnaise with grilled fish or crabcakes.

1 cup nonfat mayonnaise
1/2 cup 1/2% milk
1 clove garlic, minced
1/2 teaspoon ground cumin
1 teaspoon adobo paste from a can of chipotle peppers in adobo
Juice of one lime
1 tablespoon cilantro

Blend all ingredients in a food processor for 30 seconds.

Yield: 1 3/4 cups

5 calories / trace of fat per tablespoon

CHIPOTLE PAPAYA RELISH (FOR FISH)

Cold, yet hot. Sweet, yet tart. Served alongside grilled chicken or fish, seeming contradictions that soon elicit compliments. See the previous recipe, "Chipotle Mayonnaise", for a description of, and cautions about, chipotles.

1 teaspoon minced chipotle pepper with adobo sauce
1 papaya, peeled, seeded and diced
1/4 cup red onion, finely diced
1/4 cup red bell pepper, finely diced
1/4 cup green bell pepper, finely diced
1 teaspoon minced chives
1 teaspoon minced cilantro
1/2 cup papaya nectar
2 tablespoons rice vinegar

Combine all ingredients. Serve with grilled fish.

Yield: Approximately 3 cups

4 calories/ trace of fat per tablespoon

GREEN CHILE SAUCE

Considered a staple by many of the denizens of these parts, "Chile" finds its way to the table morning, noon and night as a condiment for eggs, potatoes, vegetables, grilled meats, etc. We like to pair it with its crimson counterpart, roasted red pepper sauce, underneath our Black Bean Tamale Casserole. See the glossary for a discussion on the roasting and peeling of peppers.

1/4 cup vegetable oil
1/2 cup onion, finely diced
2 cloves garlic, minced
2 tablespoons flour
1 cup chicken stock
1 1/2 cups green chiles (Anaheim, Concho de Toro or other long, green, semi-mild chile), roasted, peeled, seeded and diced
1 tomato, diced
1 teaspoon coriander
1 tablespoon chopped cilantro

Saute onions and garlic in oil. Whisk in flour.

Cook, stirring, for three minutes.

Whisk in heated stock. Cook five minutes.

Add remaining ingredients and cook 20 minutes.

Yield: 4 cups

10 calories / .8 grams fat per tablespoon

SIX OR SEVEN ONIONS SAUCE

An intimidating or inviting title, depending upon your inclinations. It may be used to describe either the amount and/or the variety involved. Like the members of most families, onion types are more alike than not; still each lends an indisputable contribution, with the whole being greater than the sum of its parts.

2 tablespoons olive oil
1 leek, cleaned and sliced into thin rings
1 large shallot, peeled, sliced into thin rings
1/2 cup white or yellow onion or a combination of the two, sliced into
       thin rings
6 cloves garlic, sliced paper thin
12 green onions, halved lengthwise, cut into two inch sections
1/2 cup white or red wine
1/2 cup appropriate stock (seafood, chicken, beef or vegetable)
2 tablespoons parsley, chopped
2 tablespoons chives, minced

Warm olive oil in a large skillet. Add leek, shallot, white and yellow onion, and garlic. Saute briefly, then cover and cook over very low heat for 10 minutes.

Add green onions and appropriate stock, reduce rapidly to glaze.

Stir in parsley and chives. Serve over grilled meats or vegetables.

Yield: 3 1/2 cups

9 calories / .6 grams fat per tablespoon

CHIPOTLE SALSA

If you've been paying attention, you may have gathered by now, judging from the number of times it appears as an ingredient in this book, that we have a fondness for the chipotle pepper that borders on preoccupation. Such a suspicion would not be misplaced. Try this spicy, smoky salsa over enchiladas or tacos or as an accompaniment to grilled meats.

1/2 medium onion, sliced
1 clove garlic, minced
2 teaspoons vegetable oil
1 tablespoon brown sugar
1-1/2 cups canned tomato sauce
1/2 cup water
2 tablespoons adobo paste from canned chipotle peppers
2 teaspoons lime juice

Saute onion and garlic in oil until softened.

Puree all ingredients in a food processor, and simmer for 10 minutes. Add lime juice.

Yield: 2 1/2 cups

7.5 calories/ .25 grams fat per tablespoon

MOCK HOLLANDAISE

True Hollandaise may be one of the world's great sauces, but it is tricky to make, harder to keep, and comprised almost entirely of egg yolks and butter, so we will spend little time apologizing for this delightful imitation which is shamefully easy to construct, keeps for a week, is fat free, and tastes great. Use it warm or cold, as a sauce or a dip. See the next page for variations of this basic premise.

3/4 cup fat free mayonnaise
1/2 cup 1/2% milk
Dash of white pepper
Dash of cayenne pepper
1 1/2 teaspoons lemon zest
2 tablespoons lemon juice
1/4 teaspoon yellow food coloring (optional)

Combine first four ingredients in a small saucepan. Cook for three minutes over low heat, stirring constantly. Stir in remaining ingredients and serve immediately.

Serve over steamed vegetables, grilled fish or eggs.

Yield: 1 1/4 cups

20 calories / .2 grams fat per 2 tablespoon serving

Contributed by Trisha Shirey

VARIATIONS ON MOCK HOLLANDAISE

These are, of course, just a few of the myriad variations possible. They all have in common the mayonnaise and a bit of acid, (citric or vinegar), but after that, anything goes. Feel free to make up your own combinations; and if you like the results, name it after yourself: Sauce "whoever". Just send us the recipe.

ORANGE HOLLANDAISE: Reduce lemon juice to 1 tablespoon, add 2 tablespoons orange juice, orange zest, 1 teaspoon orange juice concentrate.

DILLED DIJON HOLLANDAISE: Add 1 tablespoon minced fresh dill and 2 tablespoons of dijon mustard.

LIME HOLLANDAISE: Simply substitute equal amounts of lime juice and zest for lemon.

BEARNAISE: Substitute 2 tablespoons tarragon or Mexican marigold mint vinegar for lemon juice, add 1 tablespoon freshly minced tarragon or marigold mint.

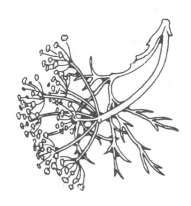

MOCK SOUR CREAM

This popular sauce has been reprinted from Spa Specialties. It is easy to make, keeps well, is free from artificial flavorings and preservatives and is lower in fat than most commercial low fat sour creams. Great on baked potatoes and with a variety of Mexican foods.

1 cup low fat cottage cheese
1 tablespoon lemon juice
1/4 cup skim milk (optional)

Combine cottage cheese and lemon juice in a blender or food processor. Process until smooth. Add milk to thin to desired consistency. Refrigerate.

Yield: 1 1/4 cups

9.5 calories / .12 grams fat per 1 tablespoon serving

HONEY LIME GARLIC GLAZE

Largely responsible for the "Honey Lime Garlic Craze" now sweeping across the condiments; also descriptive of the look partakers assume soon after consuming same. Addictive enough to merit a cautionary label.

1/3 cup freshly squeezed lime juice
2 tablespoons honey
4 cloves garlic, minced
1/2 fresh jalapeño (or other hot green pepper), seeded and minced
1/2 dried chipotle pepper, seeded and soaked in water (or canned chipotle
      in adobo; available in some grocery stores)
1/4 teaspoon cornstarch
1 tablespoon cilantro, chopped

Combine the first six ingredients in a blender. Puree. Pour the contents into a small saucepan and bring to a simmer over medium heat, stirring occasionally. Reduce until slightly thickened; remove from heat and stir in cilantro.

Use as a basting glaze and sauce for grilled chicken or fish. Or, try it as a dip for chilled shrimp, vegetable crudities, and, as a last resort, your index finger.

Chipotle peppers are hot! Use accordingly when making this spicy sweet and sour condiment.

Yield: 2/3 cup

13 calories/ 0 grams fat per tablespoon

LIME MUSTARD SAUCE

This is one of those great recipes that probably takes longer to write down than it does to make. You will find it is an "instant" success over grilled seafood or chicken.

1 pint fat free mayonnaise
1/2 cup Dijon mustard
1/2 cup lime juice, freshly squeezed
1 tablespoon fresh dill, minced (or 1 1/2 teaspoons dried)

Combine all ingredients and chill.

Yield: 3 cups

11 calories/ trace of fat per tablespoon

MANGO SALSA

Sassy sun colored salsas, such as this one spun from mango and lime, lend a bright festive touch to almost any food. We particularly like them with grilled or smoked poultry and fish. If fresh mangoes are unavailable, bottled ones, rinsed of their syrup, make an excellent substitute; or try chunk pineapple in its own juice.

2 cups fresh ripe mango, diced
2 tablespoons lime juice
1 serrano pepper, seeded and finely chopped
1 clove garlic, minced
1 tablespoon fresh cilantro, minced

Combine all ingredients and refrigerate for at least one hour before serving.

Yield: 2 1/4 cups

7 calories/ trace of fat per tablespoon

Contributed by Trisha Shirey

PICO DE GALLO

Pico de Gallo translates as "chicken beak" which I surmise alludes to its color and the idea that it should be just 'picante' enough to give you a little 'peck'. Using fresh tomatoes and cutting the vegetables by hand (rather than using a food processor) are essential to insure the characteristic crunch and flavor of this traditional condiment for grilled meats and seafood.

1 ripe tomato, diced
1/4 onion, diced
1/2 clove garlic, minced
1/2 serrano pepper, minced
1 tablespoon chopped cilantro
Juice of 1/2 lime

Combine ingredients and chill.

Yield: 1 1/4 cups

3 calories / trace of fat per tablespoon

SALSA VERDE

This is a classic Mexican table sauce that we serve most often with our summer squash torta (page 162), but it is equally delicious drizzled over any grilled meat, poultry, seafood or as a cheese enchilada sauce. Tomatillos are available in the produce section of most grocery stores.

1 large poblano pepper, charred*, peeled and seeded
2 cups tomatillos, peeled (see the Glossary if you require tomatillo
      tutoring)
1 small onion, chopped
2 cloves garlic, minced
2 cups water
1 teaspoon cumin
Pinch of sugar
1/4 cup cilantro
Juice of 1/2 lime

Simmer tomatillos, onion and garlic in a small saucepan with water for three minutes. Drain and reserve water for thinning sauce, if necessary.

Puree the blanched vegetables in a blender or food processor with the remaining ingredients.

Use as is, or strain through a wire mesh strainer, pushing through as many solids as possible, for a smoother sauce.

Yield: 3 cups

10 calories / trace of fat per tablespoon

*Peppers are charred to remove their "cellophane-like" outer skin. Blister and blacken the outer skin of the chile in a broiler or by securing with tongs over an open flame. Plunge into ice water, then peel away the exterior skin.

ROASTED LEMON GARLIC SAUCE

Roasting the garlic gives it a deep, rich, mellow flavor. If you are a garlic lover, and you should be, save a little to spread on a thin slice of French bread and eat as is.

If you are fortunate enough to have access to some Hoja Santa leaves, try wrapping your chicken or fish in them before grilling and then top with the finished sauce.

3 large whole heads of garlic
1 tablespoon olive oil
2 tablespoons lemon juice
2 teaspoons white wine vinegar
1 tablespoon soy sauce
Freshly ground black pepper
Pinch of sugar

Remove the papery outer shell from garlic. Brush each head with oil and wrap each separately in aluminum foil. Bake at 400 degrees for 45 minutes. Let cool ten minutes.

Separate cloves; squeeze to extract pulp. Combine pulp with remaining ingredients and blend in food processor.

Serve over grilled chicken or fish.

Yield: 2/3 cup

43 calories / .7 grams fat per tablespoon

RED CHILE TARTAR SAUCE

The chili powder is, of course, a prejudicial embellishment by those of us who notion that most things, including some desserts, are improved with a bit of chile. It does provide a nice color contrast for the Blue Cornmeal Battered Trout on page 211.

2/3 cups nonfat mayonnaise
1/3 cup nonfat yogurt
1/4 cup dill pickle relish
2 tablespoons fresh dill, chopped
2 teaspoons horseradish
2 teaspoons Dijon mustard
1 tablespoon capers, drained and chopped
2 teaspoons chili powder

Combine all ingredients and chill.

Yield: Approximately 1 1/2 cups

5 calories / trace of fat per tablespoon

ROASTED RED PEPPER SAUCE

Try this brick red, earthy Southwestern salsa over the eggplant enchiladas on page 151, under a chile relleno, or with grilled meats or fish. Charring the tomatoes, onion and pepper over an open flame gives this sauce its unmistakable, and enduring, rustic character.

2 tomatoes, charred*
1 small onion, thickly sliced and charred*
1 serrano pepper, halved and seeded and charred*
1 large red bell pepper, roasted, peeled and seeded*
3 cloves garlic
2 tablespoons cilantro
Juice of 1/2 lime
1 teaspoon ground cumin

Combine all ingredients in a food processor or blender and process until smooth.

Yield: 2 cups

9 calories/ trace of fat per tablespoon

*See Glossary of Cooking Terms for directions on charring.

SALSA PICANTE

Just this last year the folks who keep track of such things officially declared picante sauce as the number one condiment in the United States, surpassing catsup, mayonnaise, mustard, and the lot. The most amazing thing about this statistic, outside of the fact that it took 'em so long, is that most people have never even had the good stuff! Almost all commercially bottled hot sauces have to be cooked, for shelf-life reasons; and consequently they lack all the vitality, fresh taste and crunch that a homemade salsa delivers. So make your own! This recipe is at its very, very best the day it is made, but would keep in the refrigerator for about a week, if you let it, which you won't. Good fresh tomatoes, when you can get them, instead of the canned make the very best of all salsas. Try either version with the fat free baked chips on page 35.

1 14 ounce can of tomatoes with juice (or 4 fresh)
1/4 onion, coarsely chopped
2 green onions, coarsely chopped
1 large clove of garlic, chopped
2 tablespoons tomato puree (optional)
3 tablespoons fresh cilantro, chopped
2 serrano peppers, chopped
juice from 1/2 lime
pinch of sugar
pinch of salt

Pulse all ingredients in a food processor to the desired consistency.

Yield: Approximately 3 cups

3 calories / trace of fat per tablespoon

TARTAR SAUCE

An additional squeeze of lemon, it must be noted, will serve the purpose of making tarter, "tartar sauce".

2/3 cup non fat mayonnaise
1/3 cup non fat yogurt
1/4 cup cornichons or other good dill pickle, chopped
2 tablespoons chopped fresh dill
2 teaspoons horseradish
2 teaspoons Dijon mustard
1 tablespoon capers, rinsed, drained and chopped

Combine all ingredients. Chill for one hour.

Yield: 1 1/2 cups

5 calories / trace of fat per tablespoon

TOMATILLO SAUCE

In addition to providing substantial nutrition and flavor, the sesame seeds serve as the binder for this wonderfully versatile, traditional style "pipian verde" from the interior of Mexico. Serve warm as an accompaniment to grilled or baked seafood (salmon is particularly good) and meats; or chilled as a dunk for chips and vegetables.

1/3 cup hulled sesame seeds
2 teaspoons corn oil
12 tomatillos, husked and rinsed
1 or 2 serrano peppers
1 cup chopped onion
2 cloves garlic, chopped
2 cups chicken stock

Optional (but authentic, and tasty)
1 sprig epazote
1 small leaf from either an avocado or hoja santa

Toast the sesame seeds until lightly golden in a heavy dry skillet over medium heat.

Cool, then pulverize in a food processor, stopping before they turn to paste.

Heat the oil in the same skillet and saute the ground seeds until golden brown.

Simmer the remaining ingredients in the stock for ten minutes, add the sesame seeds and simmer for an additional twenty minutes.

Puree all thoroughly, then press out through a coarse sieve, using the back of a large spoon to force the solids through.

Yield: Approximately 1 quart

40 calories / 4 grams fat per 1/4 cup serving

TROPICAL BARBECUE SAUCE

Put yourself on island time with a Barbadoan style barbecue. Toss a green salad, set some foil wrapped ears of corn out on the grill, skewer up some shrimp or fish, some chicken and maybe some pork tenderloin to baste with this sauce ... and Oh, Mon! you be sailin' now.

1 cup molasses
1/2 cup cider vinegar
4 tablespoons worcestershire
2 tablespoons Dijon mustard
1 teaspoon PickaPeppa sauce
1/4 cup orange juice

Combine all ingredients thoroughly in a food processor. Use to baste and sauce grilled chicken or pork tenderloin.

Yield: 2 cups

28 calories / trace of fat per tablespoon

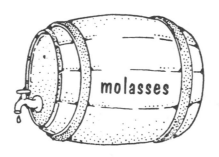

Soups

CHILLED CUCUMBER AND CHIVE SOUP

Creamy, light and refreshing, this soup is perfect for those long hot days of summer. Take the extra time to hand cut the vegetables for best results.

We recommend peeling the cucumbers unless they are organically grown and unwaxed.

1 1/2 cups mock sour cream (page 72)
2 cups buttermilk
1 cucumber, partially peeled, seeded and diced
1/2 cup parsley, chopped
1/3 cup diced red radishes
1/4 cup chives, minced
Freshly ground black pepper to taste

Combine all ingredients and chill.

Yield: 6 servings

55 calories / 1 gram fat per 6 ounce serving

COLD POTATO SOUP

In much of Europe, leeks are as commonly used as yellow or white onions are here. They will lend an unmistakable character to the finished product.

To clean dirt and sand from leeks, remove the roots and most of the darker green leaves. Cut the remaining green portion in half lengthwise. Turn the leek and make another cut lengthwise, creating an x - shaped cut in the stem. Hold the leek under running water to remove the soil between the leaves.

Often the roots of fresh leeks can be planted in the garden to start your own leek garden. Reserve at least one half inch of leek with the roots, and sprout in shallow water or plant in rich garden soil. Leeks will go dormant for a portion of the year and may be harvested in the spring. They are a good companion plant for roses and other flowers and vegetables.

2 pounds potatoes, peeled and sliced
2 cups defatted chicken stock
1 bunch leeks, cleaned and sliced (use the white part and only a small
     amount of the light green stem)
2 cups 2 % milk
1 can evaporated skim milk
1/4 teaspoon cayenne pepper
1/8 teaspoon salt
Minced fresh chives for garnish

Simmer potatoes and leeks in chicken stock until tender. Puree. Add remaining ingredients and chill.

Garnish each serving generously with fresh chives.

Yield: 12 servings

117 calories / .45 grams fat per 6 ounce serving

GAZPACHO

The color and crunch of this soup make it a natural for a light summer lunch or brunch. It tastes even better the next day, so make a day in advance of the party. Serve with a crusty French bread.

For a festive touch, set the bowl of gazpacho inside a larger bowl filled with ice and decorate the top of the ice with fresh herbs and flowers.

46 ounce can of tomato juice (may be low sodium)
2 small cucumbers, peeled and seeded
1 clove garlic, peeled
2 cloves of fresh garlic, minced
3 green onions, minced
1/2 cup onion, finely chopped
1/2 cup purple onion, finely chopped
1 small green pepper, diced
1 rib of celery, diced
3 tomatoes, diced
1 tablespoon minced fresh dill
1 tablespoon olive oil
2 teaspoons tabasco
Juice of one lime
1/4 cup red wine herbal vinegar (chive and dill would be nice)

Dice one of the cucumbers and puree the other cucumber with one of the garlic cloves.

Combine all ingredients in a large glass bowl and chill well.

Yield: 12 servings

54 calories / 1.2 grams fat per 1 cup serving

FRESH TOMATO SOUP

Set aside your ripest, reddest tomatoes for this silky, sophisticated summer soup.

One teaspoon of dried thyme may be substituted for fresh thyme, but fresh basil and parsley are essential for this recipe. Reconstitute the dried thyme in the milk for at least fifteen minutes.

3 large tomatoes, quartered
1 medium onion, sliced
1 clove garlic, minced
1 1/4 cups chicken stock
2 tablespoons tomato paste
1/4 cup chopped parsley
1/4 cup chopped fresh basil
1 tablespoon minced fresh thyme
2/3 cup 2% milk
Freshly ground black pepper to taste

Simmer tomato, onion and garlic with stock and tomato paste for fifteen minutes.

Cool slightly and puree.

Add remaining ingredients and chill.

Yield: 6 servings

45 calories / .75 grams fat per 6 ounce serving

BEAN SOUP WITH CHIPOTLE PEPPERS

Chipotle peppers are actually smoked jalapeño peppers. Yes, they are hot, but used in moderation, they impart a unique flavor and earthy richness that make this soup special. Mas picosa - mejor sabrosa.

Chipotle peppers are available in dried form or canned in adobo sauce in many grocery stores and health food stores. Check the Mexican specialty foods area of your store.

1/2 pound pinto beans
1/2 pound red or kidney beans
About one quart of defatted chicken stock
1/2 teaspoon salt
1 tablespoon olive oil
1 cup chopped onion
4 cloves garlic, minced
1 tablespoon cumin powder
1 chipotle pepper, dried or canned
Additional liquid (stock or water) to thin soup to desired consistency
Grated low fat cheddar cheese

Carefully wash the beans and cover with sufficient stock to have three inches of liquid above beans. Simmer partially covered until tender, about one and one half hours adding more liquid if necessary. Add the chipotle pepper to the beans the final thirty minutes of cooking time.

Saute the onion and garlic in oil until soft.

Remove the chipotle pepper from the beans and puree two thirds of the beans along with the onions and garlic,in a food processor or blender. Combine the puree with the remaining beans.

Add the salt, cumin, and additional liquid, if necessary, to thin.

Garnish with a sprinkle of low fat cheddar cheese.

Yield: Approximately one gallon
67 calories / .25 grams fat per 6 ounce serving

BLACK BEAN SOUP WITH JALAPEÑO SHERRY

This soup, despite it's rather menacing moniker, is not really that spicy. The peppers are strained out and the sherry imparts a subtle nutty sweetness to this hearty puree. Like most bean soups, it freezes well.

1/2 cup dry sherry
1 fresh jalapeño pepper or 3 fresh serrano peppers, seeded
1 pound black beans
1 quart water or defatted chicken stock (stock gives richer flavor)
1/2 teaspoon salt
1 tablespoon olive oil
1 cup chopped red onion
4 cloves garlic, minced
1 tablespoon cumin powder
Additional liquid as needed to thin to desired consistency

Place the sherry and the peppers in a small saucepan. Bring to a boil, then set aside.

Saute the onion and garlic in the oil until soft.

Cover the beans with sufficient liquid to have three inches of liquid above the beans. Cover and simmer until tender, about one and one half hours. Puree two thirds of the beans and the onions and garlic in a food processor or blender. Combine the pureed beans with the remaining beans.

Remove the peppers from the sherry and discard them. Add the sherry, cumin and salt.

Serve hot, garnished with a dollop of mock sour cream, if desired. (Page 72.)

Yield: Approximately one gallon

133 calories / 1.5 grams fat per 6 ounce serving

BEAN AND LEEK CHOWDER

Just the right stuff to help you get a legume up for the rigors of a winter day.

3/4 pound dried navy beans
1 1/2 tablespoons margarine
1 onion, chopped
2 carrots, diced
2 potatoes, peeled and diced
1 pound leeks, sliced (white and pale green portions only)
2 cups water
1 1/2 cups 2% milk
1/4 teaspoon cayenne pepper
Chopped parsley to garnish

Cook the beans in enough water to cover by three inches until tender and reserve.

Saute the onion and carrots in margarine. Add the leeks and potatoes and cook for five minutes. Add water and simmer until vegetables are tender.

Add beans and remaining ingredients and heat thoroughly.

Yield: 12 servings

94 calories / 1.4 grams fat per serving

LIMA BEAN SOUP

The perfect venue for the too oft maligned lima, this buttery, robust soup is quick and easy to make, yet it tastes like you spent hours in the kitchen.

12 ounces frozen lima beans
2 cups defatted chicken stock
1 clove garlic, minced
1/3 cup diced onion
1/2 teaspoon thyme
1/2 teaspoon oregano
Freshly ground black pepper

Simmer all together until beans are tender. Puree two thirds of the mixture in a food processor or blender and then return to the pot. Add to the soup:

1/2 cup diced onion
1/2 cup diced celery
1/2 cup diced carrot
1/2 cup diced bell pepper
1 clove garlic, minced

Simmer until the vegetables are just done. Thin with additional stock as needed.

Serve hot, garnished with minced chives.

Yield: 10 servings

149 calories / .75 grams fat per 6 ounce serving

MIXED BEAN SOUP

You may have noticed that many of the soups is this book begin with "a bean". This reflects not only a philosophical/nutritional bent (that there is nothing more simple, more humble, more commonplace, and yet more versatile and gastronomically virtuous than the bean); but also the fortunately widely shared prejudice that they make the most satisfying soups.

So, going on the theory that, "if a little is good, more is better", we offer you this recipe that utilizes whatever beans you may have on hand. Be creative; the results may never be the same, but I guarantee they will always be good.

1 bell pepper, diced
2 cups canned diced tomatoes, in juice
6 cloves garlic, minced
1 large onion, diced
6 cups defatted chicken stock
3 cups assorted dried beans (we use red, pinto, white, black, split green
        peas and red lentils)
2 fresh tomatoes, quartered
1 teaspoon basil
1 teaspoon oregano
1 teaspoon celery seed
1/2 teaspoon cumin
1 tablespoon tamari sauce
1/8 teaspoon cayenne
1/4 teaspoon black pepper

Combine all ingredients and simmer until beans are tender.

Add more hot stock if needed.

Puree half of the mixture to thicken, recombine and serve hot.

Yield: 20 servings

75 calories / .5 grams fat per 6 ounce serving

RED BEAN AND SAUSAGE SOUP

We stole the idea for this recipe from some friends who own a fine local restaurant, The Inn at Brushy Creek. I don't know who they stole it from. You steal it from us. (It's too good a thing not to keep going).

2 cups cooked red beans
1 teaspoon olive oil
1 cup onion, diced
3 cloves garlic, minced
6 cups chicken or beef stock (or a mixture)
2 cups cabbage, diced
1/2 cup catsup
4 new potatoes, quartered
1 tablespoon brown sugar
1 tablespoon vinegar
Freshly ground black pepper
1/2 pound sliced Carabeef* sausage

Saute onion and garlic in oil.

Add stock, cabbage, catsup and new potatoes. Cook until potatoes are almost done.

Add remaining ingredients and heat thoroughly.

Yield: 20 servings

97 calories / 1.8 grams fat per 6 ounce serving

*Carabeef is the trade name for naturally raised water buffalo which is ounce for ounce leaner than boneless, skinless chicken breast. It is available at Whole Foods Markets. Any lean sausage may be substituted.

(CAN'T BE) BEET SOUP

This rich, vibrantly hued soup makes an excellent first course for a winter's Sunday night supper featuring salmon croquettes. (See page 219.)

1 tablespoon olive oil
5 large beets, peeled and grated
1 onion, chopped
1/2 head cabbage, shredded
2 carrots, diced
2 cloves garlic, minced
2 quarts chicken or beef stock (or a combination)
1 cup tomato puree
1 tablespoon lemon juice
Black pepper

In a large soup pot, saute vegetables briefly in oil. Add the remaining ingredients and simmer until vegetables are tender.

Serve with a dollop of mock sour cream. (See page 72.)

Yield: 20 servings

90 calories / .4 grams fat per serving

CARROT AND PARSNIP SOUP
WITH ROASTED GARLIC

You will want to roast several heads of garlic. The extras make a great low fat garlic spread when the cloves are squeezed onto toasted bread or crackers.

1 large head garlic
Vegetable cooking spray

Remove papery outer shell of garlic, spray with vegetable spray, wrap in foil and roast at 400 degrees for 45 minutes, until slightly soft. Allow to cool.

1 tablespoon margarine
1 1/2 pounds carrots, sliced
3/4 pound parsnips, sliced
3 medium leeks, chopped (whites and a little green)
2 teaspoons thyme
7 1/2 cups chicken stock
Chopped parsley for garnish

Saute vegetables in margarine and vegetable cooking spray until they begin to soften. Add thyme, saute one minute.

Add stock and simmer until vegetables are done.

Squeeze garlic puree from the baked head, then blend all in a food processor. Serve hot or cold garnished with chopped parsley.

Yield: 16 servings

68 calories / .4 grams fat per serving

CARROT AND SWEET POTATO SOUP

The ancho chile gives this "burnt orange" bisque a special depth and pungency. You can find dried anchoes in the produce section of most grocery stores in the Southwest.

2 tablespoons vegetable oil
1/2 cup chopped onion
2 tablespoons garlic, minced
1 1/2 cups peeled, chopped carrots
1 cup white wine
3 medium sweet potatoes, peeled and chopped
1 ancho chile, stemmed and seeded
1 tablespoon cumin
1 quart chicken stock
Pinch of salt
Freshly ground black pepper
1 cup 2 % milk

Saute onions in oil until softened. Add the garlic and saute for one minute.

Simmer all vegetables and seasonings in wine and stock until tender. Drain off and reserve some of the liquid and puree the solids in a blender or food processor to a smooth consistency. Combine with the reserved liquid, add the milk and heat thoroughly.

Yield: 12 servings

117 calories / 1.2 grams fat per serving

SMOKED CORN CHOWDER

I don't know that I would go to all the trouble of firing up my smoker just to make this soup (I might though, this stuff is good!); but the next time you <u>are</u> using the grill, remember three things: smoked corn would probably go well with whatever you are serving, it doesn't hurt to throw on a few extra ears, and while you're at it, why not hunt up the Smoked Tomato Sauce recipe in this book and go all out? (page 150)

6 ears of corn, smoked
1/2 large onion, diced
3 cloves garlic, minced
1 1/2 teaspoons vegetable oil
3 cups defatted chicken stock
1 large potato, peeled and diced
1 small red bell pepper, roasted, peeled and diced*
1 small poblano pepper, roasted, peeled and diced*
1 cup 2% milk
1/2 teaspoon oregano
1/2 teaspoon cumin
Thinly sliced "Carabeef" sausage for garnish**

Smoke the corn in the husks for at least one hour in your barbecue smoker. Cut the corn from the cobs.

Simmer the cobs in the chicken stock for thirty minutes, then remove and discard.

Saute the onion and garlic in oil until softened. Add the stock, potatoes and corn. Simmer until the potatoes are done, about twenty minutes.

Puree half of the mixture in a food processor or blender. Add to the remaining soup. Then add the milk, peppers and seasonings. Simmer on low heat for ten minutes and serve hot.

Yield: 10 servings

94 calories / 1.4 grams fat per 6 ounce serving

*See Glossary for directions for roasting peppers.

**Carabeef is the trade name for sausage made from ultra-lean water buffalo which are fed hormone and preservative free foods on a ranch in Arkansas. This sausage is available through most Whole Foods Markets. Any low fat link sausage may be substituted.

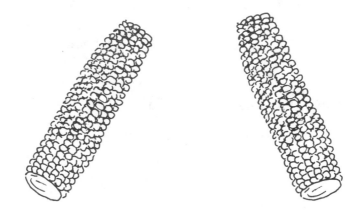

SOPA DE ELOTE (CORN SOUP)

Corn, in its many forms, is a staple in Mexico. This soup uses it twice: the actual kernels and the corn tortilla used as a thickener.

1 teaspoon vegetable oil
1 small onion, diced
3 cloves garlic, minced
2 cups frozen kernel corn, thawed
3 cups chicken stock
1 corn tortilla
1/2 teaspoon oregano
1 teaspoon cumin
1/2 cup canned diced green chiles (4 ounce can)
1/2 cup diced red bell pepper
1/8 teaspoon cayenne
Chopped fresh cilantro for garnish

Saute the onion and garlic in the oil until tender. Add the stock and corn and simmer for five minutes.

Bake or microwave the tortilla until crisp. Crumble and add to corn mixture and simmer for five more minutes.

Puree two thirds of the corn mixture in a food processor or blender. Combine with the remaining corn and add the remaining ingredients. Simmer until tender. Garnish with cilantro before serving.

Yield: 8 servings

61 calories / .4 grams fat per 6 ounce serving

CORN AND TOMATILLO SOUP

Tomatilloes are readily available in the produce section of most grocery stores, their faintly luminescent green orbs sheathed in drab, papery outer husks. (Peek to find the good ones.) This soup is a personal favorite and one that I'm sure you will want to make frequently; be advised however, there are no substitutes for either tomatilloes or fresh cilantro.

Vegetable cooking spray
1 tablespoon margarine
1 medium onion, finely chopped
6 tomatilloes, husked and chopped
1 tablespoon minced garlic
30 ounces frozen corn kernels, thawed (usually three boxes)
4 cups defatted chicken stock
1 cup frozen peas, thawed
1 tablespoon cilantro
4 ounces canned diced green chiles
1/4 cup packed, chopped fresh or frozen spinach, thawed
1 tablespoon sugar

Saute the onions, tomatilloes, and garlic in the margarine and vegetable spray.

Puree with 4 cups of the corn, 3 cups of the stock, the peas and cilantro. Place the puree in a stock pot, add chiles, spinach, sugar, remaining corn and stock. Simmer for fifteen minutes.

Garnish with baked tortilla strips (page 35), mock sour cream (page 72) and fresh cilantro.

Yield: 16 servings

86 calories / 1.6 grams fat per 6 ounce serving

GREEN CHILE SOUP

Use a large, mild green chile like Anaheim. The finished soup should have a little "smoulder" to it, but not strip the enamel off your teeth.

3 bell peppers, roasted and peeled*
3 green chiles, roasted and peeled*
1 small onion, minced
1 tablespoon cumin
2 cloves garlic, minced
1/4 cup fresh minced cilantro
4 cups chicken stock
1 cup evaporated skim milk
2 tablespoons cornstarch
Mock sour cream (page 72)

Simmer vegetables and seasonings in the stock. Puree.

Mix cornstarch with milk; add to vegetables, heat (do not boil).

Garnish with mock sour cream.

Yield: 12 servings

76 calories / .5 grams fat per serving

*See Glossary for information on roasting peppers.

LENTIL SOUP WITH CHILE AND LIME

For a lot of people, lentils are the culinary equivalent of televised professional bowling, and without getting into the merits of whether or not they deserve this lowly status among legumes, most of us would probably agree that they are at their best combined with stronger, more exotic flavors. The curried lentils on page 20 and this soup, pungent with cumin, chiles and lime, are excellent examples.

3 cups lentils
12 cups water
1 1/2 teaspoons salt
2 teaspoons black pepper
2 teaspoons cumin
2 teaspoons oregano
3 bay leaves
1/2 cup canned diced green chiles
1 large green bell pepper, finely diced
1 large carrot, finely diced
1/2 cup lime juice
1 tablespoon olive oil

Combine the first seven ingredients in a large pot. Bring to a boil, then lower heat and simmer until lentils are tender, skimming as necessary.

Puree 1/3 of this mixture, along with chiles. Return to pot along with bell pepper and carrot and cook until vegetables are just done.

Stir in the olive oil. Add the lime juice just before serving.

Yield: Approximately 3 quarts

130 calories/ 1.2 grams fat per 6 ounce serving

MEXICAN LENTIL SOUP

This tasty and slightly unusual lentil soup is a sure fire way to satisfy your weekly cactus requirements! It is actually quite good without the nopales, which are the de-thorned pads of the prickly pear cactus, but not as much fun!

1/2 pound lentils (one cup)
12 cups water
1 pound nopales, cut into small squares
2 teaspoons salt
2 large tomatoes
2 cloves garlic, minced
1 1/2 tablespoons olive oil
1/2 onion, minced
2 fresh jalapeño peppers, seeded and minced
2 tablespoons cilantro, coarsely chopped
2-3 cups chicken stock
Cilantro for garnish

Simmer the nopales in a small amount of water until tender.

Rinse lentils, then cook in water until very soft.

Puree tomatoes with garlic.

Saute onions and peppers in oil until tender. Add tomato mixture and cook, stirring, until almost dry.

Add remaining ingredients, thinning with stock as needed. Simmer for 20 minutes. Garnish with additional cilantro before serving.

Yield: 20 servings

85 calories / .75 grams fat per 6 ounce serving

GREEN OKRA GUMBO

This backwater bayou recipe will stick to your ribs. (The roux may stick to your skin, too, so be careful!) Just the stuff you need to fortify yourself before a tough day out alligator wrestling or dealing with anything involving attorneys. Most of us would take the 'gators, I suspect.

1 tablespoon vegetable oil
2 teaspoons flour
1 serrano pepper, seeded and minced
1 cup diced onion
1/3 cup diced celery
1 cup diced green bell pepper
4 cloves garlic, minced
1/4 cup brown rice
1/4 teaspoon coriander
1/4 teaspoon cayenne
8 ounces okra, sliced
1 bunch green onions, minced
1/4 cup minced parsley
1 teaspoon gumbo file powder
1 quart chicken stock

Make a dark chocolate roux with the oil and flour. (See the caution given with the Shrimp Creole recipe, page 222.)

Remove from heat and stir in serrano, onion, celery, bell pepper and garlic until slightly softened and well coated. Bring stock to a boil and stir into the roux mixture.

Add the rice and seasonings. Simmer for thirty minutes.

Briefly saute the okra in a non stick skillet and add to the soup along with the green onions and parsley. Add the file powder and serve.

Yield: 10 servings

75 calories / 1.5 grams fat per serving

PUMPKIN AND PEAR SOUP

Fall vegetables seem to have a natural affinity for their fruit counterparts. This subtle blending of pumpkin and pear is an excellent example.

Vegetable cooking spray
1 teaspoon olive oil
1 cup onion, chopped
2 cups pear nectar
1 cup peeled and diced potato
1/4 teaspoon salt
1/8 teaspoon pepper
2 cups 2% milk
1 3/4 cups pumpkin, cooked and mashed
1 teaspoon orange rind, grated
3/4 teaspoon ginger
Light sour cream
Vegetable cooking spray

Spray a pan with vegetable spray and saute onion in oil until tender.

Add pear nectar, potato and seasonings; simmer until potato is done. Puree in a food processor or blender.

Return to the pot, add remaining ingredients and heat thoroughly over low heat. Garnish with 1/2 teaspoon light sour cream.

Yield: 12 servings

90 calories / 1.2 grams fat per 6 ounce serving

SEAFOOD GUMBO

For an authentic 'back bayou' gumbo, you will want your finished roux to achieve the color and consistency of chocolate syrup, a feat which requires the combined concentration, exacting patience and simple nerve usually reserved for stalking a wounded tiger in the brush or applying eyeliner in moving traffic. Successful completion of any one of these three tasks may be considered as preparation for the other two.

3 tablespoons vegetable oil
1/4 cup flour
6 cloves garlic, minced
1-1/2 cups onion, finely diced
3/4 cup bell pepper, finely diced
3/4 cup celery, finely diced
2 quarts seafood stock
1 cup parsley, minced
1 small can of tomato paste
1 teaspoon tabasco
4 cups canned tomatoes, diced
2 small bay leaves
2 teaspoons thyme
1 pound fresh okra, sliced
vegetable cooking spray
1 tablespoon worcestershire
1-1/2 pounds assorted seafood (shrimp, fish, oysters, crabmeat) cut into
     small bite-sized pieces

Using a wooden spoon or wire whip, whisk the flour and oil together in a small, heavy skillet. Cook over medium low heat, stirring constantly, until the roux reaches the desired color. This procedure should take about 15 to 20 minutes as the roux deepens in color from blond to caramel to walnut to dark chocolate; if you are less than attentive, it will burn and you must begin again.

Have your diced onion, bell pepper, celery and garlic close at hand, and just when you think the roux cannot possibly darken any further, add them all at once. Turn off the heat and stir until all the vegetables are well coated.

Heat the stock to boiling in a large pot and whisk in the roux/vegetable mixture. Add the parsley, tomato products and seasonings and simmer for 45 minutes.

Briefly saute the sliced okra in a skillet using the spray; add to the gumbo and simmer 30 minutes. Just before serving, add the worcestershire and seafood; cook for 5 minutes and serve.

Yield: Approximately 1 1/2 gallons

60 calories / 1.5 grams fat per 3/4 cup serving

SPANISH ONION SOUP

This version is a nice twist (or is it a squeeze?) on one of the world's classic soups. You may make it ahead of time just to the point of adding the lime juice, which should be done just before serving.

1 tablespoon olive oil
2 large onions, thinly sliced, julienned or chopped
1 tablespoon sugar
1 tablespoon flour
2 cups hot rich stock (chicken, beef or vegetable)
1 tablespoon reduced sodium soy sauce
Juice and shells of one lime
1 tablespoon fresh chopped cilantro
1 teaspoon cracked black pepper
Parmesan cheese
Fat free croutons

Heat the oil in a heavy nonstick skillet. Cook the onions slowly, stirring frequently until soft and translucent and beginning to brown in color. (About 20 minutes.) It is important to cook them slowly, they will be bitter if allowed to brown too quickly.

Add sugar and stir to caramelize onions. Add the flour, stirring well as it browns.

Pour in the hot stock slowly, stirring constantly. Add the soy sauce and pepper.

Remove from heat and add the lime juice and shells of the lime. Allow the soup to stand for a few minutes, then remove and discard the lime shells. (Don't leave them in too long or the soup will be bitter.)

Garnish the soup with cilantro, croutons, and parmesan cheese.

Yield: 6 servings
79 calories / 1.5 grams fat per 6 ounce serving

Contributed by Trisha Shirey

SMOKED TOMATO SOUP WITH BASIL PESTO

This soup is a cross cultural splice from Cannes via Cancun. Maybe Mexiterreanian?

1 poblano chile pepper
6 tomatoes
1 onion
1 clove garlic, minced
1 1/4 cups chicken stock
2 tablespoons tomato paste
1 tablespoon fresh oregano, chopped
2/3 cup 2% milk
Basil Pesto (from Spa Specialties Cookbook)

Smoke tomatoes, poblano and onion in a barbecue smoker for one hour. Peel and seed the pepper.

Simmer vegetables, stock, tomato paste and oregano together for 15 minutes.

Puree, add milk and heat thoroughly. Serve with a small dollop of basil pesto.

Yield: 8 servings

64 calories / 1.2 grams fat per serving

WINTER SQUASH SOUP

Winter squash and apples are always a great paring. The curry adds a bit of intrigue.

2 butternut squash, seeded and halved
4 acorn squash, seeded and halved
1 tablespoon corn oil margarine
2 large onions, chopped
2 large apples (Macintosh), peeled, seeded and chopped
1 tablespoon curry powder
2 quarts chicken stock
Black pepper

Bake or steam squash. Remove the peels and discard.

Saute onions and apples in margarine.

Puree all ingredients. Reheat and serve warm.

Yield: 16 servings

88 calories / .8 grams fat per serving

Salad Dressings

ANCIENT GIFTS: OLIVES AND WINE
(A vignette on the virtues of vinaigrette)

Tens of centuries ago, long before Rome ruled that part of the world, Mediterranean peoples were regularly dousing seasonally collected field greens, roots, dried and fresh fruits and nuts with oil pressed from olives and vinegar distilled from wine. The intertwining medicinal, ceremonial and gastronomical virtues of these two substances trace their roots beyond written history, and their ancient, aromatic infusion, a vinaigrette, was almost certainly our first salad dressing. And, while our notions of what ingredients comprise a proper salad may have sallied about through the passage of time and taste, the construction of vinaigrette has remained remarkably sanguine. Until recently.

The rub stems from a traditional vinaigrette's consisting of three or so parts of oil to one part vinegar, an amount and proportion deemed unwise by most of us who believe that fat consumption should be limited to approximately 20% of our daily caloric intake. This is a sound philosophy, worth extolling, but one that should not suffer for lack of exception, namely this: if you would enjoy a vinaigrette upon your salad occasionally (and we believe you should), then take care to procure and employ the best ingredients available to you, and make the real thing.

If this sounds slightly heretical, be comforted that historically you are in a long line of good and numbered company. Consider also, from a contemporary perspective, that olive oil is classified as a 'mono-saturate' and that good arguments are being put forth that fats in this category may well prove, in moderate consumption, to be more healthful than their more popular cousins, the polyunsaturates. And finally, know that the new "significantly reduced fat/calorie versions" (and we have tried every one we could get our lettuce leaves on) inevitably disappoint. They introduce excessive sweetener to balance the disproportionate acid or water to dilute it; they confound the palate with a cacophony of condiments designed to disguise their underlying, fundamental weakness: they are low in fat but they are lower still in self esteem and spirit.

This is not to suggest that there are no good low fat salad dressings; quite the opposite is true. There are some excellent ones, several in this book (try the Honey Dijon Dressing for a low fat, non creamy, "vinaigrette style" dressing).

But, just every once in a while when you're of a mind to summon up the best that history and earth have to offer, take:

3 1/2 tablespoons of 'extra-virgin' olive oil (this means it is from the first pressing of olives, and best quality)
Whisk in: 1 tablespoon of a good herbal wine vinegar (we make and market several at Lake Austin Spa Resort)
Add: 1/2 clove finely minced garlic, a small pinch of dry mustard, 1 teaspoon finely minced chives, 1 teaspoon freshly minced herbs (almost any will do), a tiny pinch of salt (for humility) and a generous grinding of black pepper from the mill.

Allow this mixture to consider itself for fifteen minutes or so (so that the flavors will, out of curiosity, co-mingle) then re-whisk thoroughly before lightly tossing with enough freshly crisped and dried greens (with perhaps some good tomatoes and thinly sliced cucumber) to feed six.

70 calories / 8 grams fat per serving

Remember, the only delight greater than a new truth discovered, is an old one, re-discovered.

BUTTERMILK RANCH DRESSING

More fine victuals from the boys on the Buttermilk Ranch. This recipe lends itself readily to adaptation. Try adding an ounce of blue cheese, crumbled. Or a tablespoon of tomato paste. Or substituting a different herb. Or ...?

1 cup buttermilk
1/3 cup fat free mayonnaise
1 clove garlic, minced
1/2 teaspoon sugar
1 teaspoon fresh dill
1/4 teaspoon dry mustard
2 tablespoons chopped parsley
Freshly ground black pepper to taste

Combine all ingredients. Chill.

Yield: 1 1/2 cups

17 calories / .5 grams fat per tablespoon

CITRUS CHIPOTLE VINAIGRETTE

This zippy little lip smacker goes great with smoked chicken salad or as a dunk for raw fruits and vegetables.

4 tablespoons orange juice concentrate
2 tablespoons tangerine juice concentrate
Juice from one large lime
4 tablespoons water
2 teaspoons olive oil
1 teaspoon minced garlic
1 teaspoon Dijon mustard
1 1/2 tablespoons minced fresh basil
2 teaspoons adobo paste from canned chipotle chiles

Whisk all ingredients together thoroughly. Chill.

Yield: 1 cup

23 calories / .8 grams fat per tablespoon

CREAMY CHAMPAGNE DRESSING

Tres elegant. Tres easy. Store and pour from the empty champagne bottle.

2 tablespoons minced parsley
1/4 cup minced fresh chives
2 shallots, minced
2 teaspoons cracked mustard seed
1/2 teaspoon celery seed
1 cup flat champagne
1 cup nonfat mayonnaise
1 1/2 cups nonfat sour cream
2 tablespoons champagne vinegar
1/4 teaspoon salt
Freshly ground black pepper

Whisk all ingredients together thoroughly. Pour into a champagne bottle and chill.

Yield: 1 quart

15 calories / 0 grams fat per tablespoon

CREAMY CHEESE AND DILL DRESSING

This tastes best if you let it sit for a day before serving. Try also as a dip for raw vegetables.

1/2 cup 1% cottage cheese
2 tablespoons nonfat cream cheese, softened
1/4 cup nonfat mayonnaise
1/4 cup nonfat sour cream
2/3 cup skim milk
2 tablespoons lemon juice
1 tablespoon olive oil
1 tablespoon Dijon mustard
1 tablespoon low sodium soy sauce
1 clove garlic, minced
1 tablespoon fresh dill
Pinch of sugar
Freshly grated black pepper

Blend cottage cheese and cream cheese in a food processor. Add remaining ingredients and blend.

Yield: 2 cups

25 calories / 1 gram fat per tablespoon

CREAMY GARLIC DRESSING

The rule of thumb we operate on around here is that if it has garlic in it, it has a chance to be good!

1/2 cup nonfat sour cream
1/2 cup skim milk
2 teaspoons Spanish sherry vinegar
2 teaspoons olive oil
1 large garlic clove, minced
Pinch of salt
2 tablespoons minced fresh parsley or other herb
Freshly ground black pepper

Blend sour cream and milk together. Add vinegar and let sit for one minute. Whisk in remaining ingredients. Chill.

Yield: 1 1/4 cups

10 calories / .5 grams fat per tablespoon

DIJON VINAIGRETTE

If we had any sense we would keep this recipe as a trade secret; it's the most popular dressing at the resort by far, and deservedly so. Too good, really, not to share. You may substitute dried leaf basil for the fresh (halve the quantity and use more parsley) but it won't be quite the same. Use chives, thyme, or other fresh herbs also.

It keeps well in the refrigerator for a week.

2 cloves garlic
1/4 cup parsley sprigs, packed
1/4 cup basil leaves, packed
1/2 teaspoon cracked black pepper
1 cup Dijon mustard
1 cup balsamic vinegar
2 cups tomato juice
2 tablespoons honey

Drop garlic into food processor or blender while motor is running. Add fresh herbs and process until finely chopped. Add the remaining ingredients and mix only until blended. Chill.

Yield: 4 cups

7 calories / .2 grams fat per tablespoon

Contributed by Trisha Shirey

NEW WORLD ORDER DRESSING

This used to be called Russian dressing, but hey, things change. Great on salads or sandwiches.

1 cup buttermilk
6 tablespoons nonfat sour cream
3 tablespoons tomato paste
2 tablespoons minced shallots
1 tablespoon Dijon mustard
1 teaspoon prepared horseradish
1/2 teaspoon Worcestershire sauce
1/2 teaspoon sugar

Whisk all together thoroughly. Chill.

Yield: 1 3/4 cups

12 calories / .2 grams fat per serving

Entree Salads

SMOKED CHICKEN SALAD WITH CITRUS CHIPOTLE DRESSING

This dish teeters precipitously close to that chasm of cutesy, pseudo-Southwestern cuisine currently buzzwording its way through our culinary heritage like Clint Eastwood through a bunch of Italian stand-ins. I like it anyway, so punish me by serving it with individual black bean souffles baked in miniature barrel cacti.

1/2 cup purple onion rings
1/2 cup vinegar
1/2 cup water

To pickle onion rings: slice the onions, put in a glass bowl. Combine a half cup of vinegar and a half cup of water and bring to a boil, then pour over onions. Let steep at least 30 minutes. Use an herbal vinegar if desired.

Salad ingredients:
4 four ounce boneless, skinless, smoked chicken breasts, cut into bite-sized pieces
1 large red bell pepper, roasted, peeled, seeded and cut into strips (see the Glossary for directions on roasting and peeling)
1 large green bell pepper, roasted, peeled, seeded and cut into thin strips
1 cup fresh mango, cubed
1 cup fresh pineapple, cubed
1 cup peeled jicama, cut into match stick size pieces
1/2 cup carrots, cut into match sticks
1/2 cup Citrus Chipotle Vinaigrette (page 119)
8 ounces fresh, clean, trimmed spinach

Whisk all dressing ingredients together. Mix with the first eight salad ingredients. Serve on a bed of fresh spinach, topped with a few pickled onion rings.

Yield: 4 servings

275 calories / 4.6 grams fat per serving

'GATHERING THE GARDEN' PASTA SALAD

Feel free to improvise with the vegetable selection in this dish; we do. And remember that this is really one of those dishes only as good as its ingredients. Fresh basil is imperative; and the use of a good olive oil, freshly grated imported Parmesan cheese and olives will greatly enhance the final result. A chilled anchovy filet would not be out of place if you are so inclined.

8 ounces of tomato and basil flavored rotini pasta, cooked al dente
2 cups of mixed vegetables, chopped or sliced and lightly steamed
  (asparagus, red bell pepper, purple onion, carrots, zucchini, mushrooms,
   broccoli, tomatoes)
1 tablespoon minced fresh garlic
2 tablespoons olive oil
1 tablespoon red wine vinegar
1 cup chopped fresh basil
1 ounce Parmesan cheese
freshly ground black pepper to taste
Imported (Calamata) black olives for garnish

Combine all ingredients and chill.

Yield: 6 servings

270 calories / 5.5 grams fat per serving

SHRIMP, MANGO AND RICE SALAD

The coolness of the mayonnaise and sour cream balance the spice of the curry and cayenne; just so the tartness of the lime and the sweetness of the mango.

1/2 cup nonfat mayonnaise
1/4 cup nonfat sour cream
1 tablespoon curry powder
Juice of 1/2 lime
1 1/2 cups cooked, cold white rice
1/8 teaspoon cayenne
2 ribs celery, diced
1/2 cup diced red bell pepper
1 cup sliced water chestnuts, drained
1/4 cup minced green onion
1 pound cooked, peeled chilled shrimp
3 cups diced fresh mango
1/4 cup sliced toasted almonds

Combine the first four ingredients thoroughly in a large bowl. Mix in the next six ingredients. Serve on a lettuce leaf garnished with the almonds.

Yield: 6 servings

265 calories / 3.5 grams fat per serving

SMOKED TROUT AND PASTA SALAD

Just put a few trout filets on the grill and cover to slow cook after you finish your next outdoor barbecue and you will be all set.

The creamy citrus dressing provides a nice counter to the spinach and chilled smoked fish.

4 ounces of shell pasta, cooked according to package directions
1 pound smoked trout filets, cut into bite sized pieces
8 ounces fresh spinach, washed and trimmed
1 large red bell pepper, roasted, peeled, seeded and cut into strips (see
   the glossary for instructions)
1 cup sliced fresh mushrooms
1 cup artichoke hearts, cut into quarters
1 cucumber, peeled and cubed

Combine ingredients and toss lightly with dressing.

Dressing:
1/2 cup nonfat yogurt
1/2 cup nonfat sour cream
1 cup nonfat mayonnaise
1 teaspoon lemon zest
1 teaspoon lime zest
1 teaspoon grapefruit zest
1 tablespoon each of lemon, lime and grapefruit juice
2 tablespoons minced fresh dill
1 clove garlic, minced
1 tablespoon minced fresh parsley
1 teaspoon balsamic vinegar
1 tablespoon horseradish
1/2 teaspoon anchovy paste
Freshly ground black pepper

Combine all ingredients and mix thoroughly.

Yield: 4 servings (280 calories / 2.5 grams fat per serving)

TORTELLINI WITH SALMON SALAD

A great way to utilize leftover salmon. Tuna would work too. The Italian name for this dish is "Tortellini con Salmonella", but we were afraid something might be found in the translation!

12 ounces cheese tortellini, cooked and chilled
1 cup green peas, cooked
1/2 red bell pepper, diced
1/2 cup chopped red onion
12 ounces cooked salmon, skin and bones removed
One 14-ounce can of artichoke hearts, drained and quartered
1/2 cup chopped fresh parsley
1/4 cup chopped fresh basil

Toss all ingredients together. Dress with:

1 clove garlic, minced
1 teaspoon dijon mustard
2 tablespoons lemon juice or herbal vinegar
1/4 cup orange juice
2 tablespoons olive oil
1/4 cup nonfat yogurt
1/4 cup chopped fresh basil
Freshly ground black pepper

Mix all ingredients together thoroughly.

Yield: 6 servings

294 calories / 4.5 grams fat per serving

Vegetables

SIDE VEGETABLES

For a book produced by a kitchen that so vociferously espouses the virtues of vegetables, you will find surprisingly few recipes for same herein. That is not because we don't use lots of vegetables; we do, but rather that our approach is generally that simplest is best: we grow or purchase the absolute best produce we can find and then do as little as possible to it, usually a light steaming and maybe a sprinkling of fresh herbs, before presenting it to you. We do use a few sauces for fresh vegetables (you will find those in the Sauces section) and occasionally cook up some things that require a little more preparation; recipes follow.

ARTICHOKE-SPINACH CASSEROLE

This dish makes a nice accompaniment and color contrast to any tomato based dish. Great for a "pot luck" contribution, too.

1 teaspoon olive oil
Olive oil cooking spray
2 cloves garlic, minced
12 ounces canned artichoke hearts, drained, rinsed and chopped
8 cups fresh spinach, cleaned and trimmed
Pinch cayenne pepper
Pinch nutmeg
2 ounces low fat cheddar
3 tablespoons fat free mayonnaise
1 egg
2 egg whites

Saute garlic in oil. Saute artichoke and spinach, stirring constantly until spinach is just wilted and dark green, using oil and spray.

Beat mayonnaise and egg products together, combine with spinach, then fold all ingredients into a sprayed baking dish.

Bake at 375 degrees for 25 minutes.

Yield: 8 servings

51 calories / 2.5 grams fat per serving

CORN CUSTARD

This colorful creamy casserole pairs nicely with many of our Mexican style offerings. Serve with Seafood Veracruzano and black beans for a striking combination of colors and flavors.

1 tablespoon margarine, melted
1 teaspoon flour
1/4 teaspoon dry mustard
1/2 teaspoon cayenne pepper
2 teaspoons minced green onions
1 teaspoon minced fresh parsley
2 cups whole kernel corn (thawed if frozen)
2 egg whites
1 cup nonfat sour cream
Vegetable cooking spray

Blend margarine with flour. Combine all ingredients and spread into a casserole sprayed with vegetable spray. Bake at 325 degrees for 30 minutes.

Yield: 3 1/2 cups

77 calories / 1.4 grams fat per 1/2 cup serving

SOUTHERN STYLE GREENS

Many guests are surprised to find that they like this dish. Greens are an excellent source of iron, calcium and vitamins.

1 bunch collard, mustard, kale or turnip greens (or a combination)
1 small onion, diced
2 cloves garlic, minced
1 tablespoon olive oil
1 tablespoon balsamic vinegar
2 teaspoons low sodium soy sauce
Black pepper to taste

Wash the greens carefully to remove sand and grit. Remove large or tough stems and chop the greens coarsely. In a large pot, heat the oil and saute the onion and garlic until translucent, about five to seven minutes. Add the greens and cover the pot. Stir gently every three to four minutes. Cook 7-10 minutes and remove from heat. Add vinegar, soy sauce and pepper.

Yield: 4 servings

79 calories / 1.5 grams fat per 1/2 cup serving

Optional: Omit olive oil and fry 2-3 slices of chopped bacon or turkey bacon. Remove the bacon from the oil and proceed as above. Top the greens with bacon bits before serving.

Contributed by Trisha Shirey (who grew up eating these frequently)

POTATOES AL CALDERO

This robust, satisfying dish makes an excellent focal point for a meal featuring larger portions of vegetables along with a smaller portion of roasted or grilled meat.

3 potatoes, peeled and sliced 1/8-inch thick
2 teaspoons olive oil
1 small crusty, stale dinner roll
1 clove garlic
1/4 cup diced red bell pepper
1/4 cup diced green bell pepper
2 tablespoons chopped onion
1 small tomato, cored, seeded and diced
1/2 bay leaf
1/8 teaspoon clove
1/2 teaspoon cumin
1/8 teaspoon cayenne pepper
1/8 teaspoon white pepper
1/2 teaspoon paprika
Pinch of salt
Pinch of sugar
Chopped parsley

Brush a baking dish with 1 teaspoon of the olive oil. Overlap the potatoes in a single layer; bake at 425 degrees for 20 minutes on top shelf. Turn the potatoes with a spatula and repeat. Set aside.

Cut the roll into 3 to 4 slices, brush with 1 teaspoon oil and bake until browned.

Saute bell peppers and onion in 1/2 teaspoon oil. Add 2 tablespoons of water, and cook until the water is evaporated. Add the tomatoes and seasonings and cook until softened. Remove the bay leaf.

Soak the bread in 1 1/4 cups water for five minutes. Puree the bread and vegetables and strain. Pour over the potatoes and heat before serving.

Yield: 6 servings

98 calories / 2 grams fat per serving

SPINACH SAUTE

The quick stir fry of the spinach gives an intense, dark green color and excellent texture. Add the cheese only as you serve or it will stick to the skillet. For an interesting variation, omit the mushrooms and cheese, substituting some minced onion and a few golden raisins that have been softened in hot water.

1 pound fresh spinach, cleaned and stemmed
2 teaspoons olive oil
1 cup sliced mushrooms
1 teaspoon minced garlic
2 tablespoons Parmesan cheese
Freshly ground black pepper

Heat the oil in a non stick skillet over moderately high heat. Add the mushrooms and garlic and saute, stirring.

Add the spinach and cook, folding over until the spinach is wilted.

Remove from heat, add the cheese and top with pepper to taste. Serve immediately.

Yield: 6 servings

32 calories / 2 grams fat per serving

STUFFED SQUASH

Almost any summer squash responds well to this treatment: try zucchini, tatuma, or any of the other varietals. Feel free to create your own filling combinations.

6 sunburst or patty pan squash, hollowed out
1 tablespoon corn oil margarine
1 cup finely diced onion
2 cloves garlic, minced
1 serrano pepper, seeded and minced
1/2 cup finely diced red bell pepper
1 cup frozen corn, thawed
1/2 teaspoon oregano
1/2 teaspoon dill
1 teaspoon minced parsley or cilantro
vegetable cooking spray

Steam the squash for ten minutes. Remove and discard the seeds.

Saute the onion, garlic and peppers in margarine until slightly softened. Add the corn and saute for five minutes. Add seasonings.

Use this mixture to stuff the squash. Spray a baking dish with the cooking spray and bake the squash at 375 degrees for 15 minutes.

Yield: 12 servings

32 calories / .2 grams fat per serving

SCALLOPED SWEET POTATOES AND APPLES

I am thinking about writing a cookbook devoted to all the simple, delicious ways to prepare sweet potatoes that do not include melted marshmallows as part of the recipe. This will be in it.

2 sweet potatoes, peeled and sliced
2 cooking apples (Rome, Macintosh, Winesap), peeled and sliced
1 cup orange juice
Zest from one orange
1 teaspoon cinnamon
Vegetable cooking spray

Alternate layers of sweet potato and apple in a sprayed baking dish.

Combine the orange juice, orange zest and cinnamon and pour over the sweet potatoes and apples.

Bake at 375 degrees for 40 minutes.

Yield: 6 servings

79 calories / .6 grams fat per serving

GRILLED SWEET POTATOES

They're not just for Thanksgiving anymore! Sweet potatoes are one of those highly nutritious, colorful foods that need to find their way onto our plates more often. This island-style version goes great with just about any grilled meat, chicken or fish.

3 tablespoons low sodium soy sauce
2 tablespoons water
2 tablespoons sherry
2 tablespoons honey
1 clove garlic, minced
2 pounds sweet potatoes, peeled and cut into wedges
2 teaspoons sesame oil
Vegetable cooking spray

Combine the first five ingredients.

Steam the sweet potatoes for 10 minutes. Brush with sesame oil.

Grill, basting with soy mixture, until glazed and grill marked.

Yield: 8 servings

75 calories / 1 gram fat per 4 ounce serving

WHITE BEAN GRATINEE

Equally at home along side Coq au Vin or simply with cornbread and a salad. Try with diced cooked chicken, green chiles and maybe some sliced tomatoes on top for a quick one dish meal.

1 teaspoon olive oil
3/4 cup diced onion
2 cloves garlic, minced
6 cups cooked white beans
1 cup grated low fat cheddar cheese
1/2 teaspoon cayenne pepper
1/4 cup Parmesan cheese
Vegetable cooking spray

Saute the onion and garlic in olive oil until soft. Combine with the beans, cheddar and cayenne pepper.

Spray a baking dish with vegetable spray and fill with bean mixture, top with Parmesan and bake at 375 degrees for 30 minutes.

Yield: 8 cups

125 calories / 3.3 grams fat per 1/2 cup serving

Vegetarian Entrees

BLACK BEAN SOPES

Sopes are commonly served as an appetizer in Mexico, and you may want to make small ones for this purpose. The larger version makes a delicious and unusual lunch, bursting forth with a wide array of colors, textures and flavors. You can prepare all of the salad ingredients ahead of time; the masa cakes will taste best if recently made and kept warm. (Pickle onions by slicing into a glass or stainless steel bowl and pouring a 50/50 mixture of boiling vinegar and water over them. Steep one hour and drain.)

1 tablespoon chili powder
2 teaspoons garlic powder
3 cups corn masa (available in the flour section of your grocery store)
Pinch of salt
3 tablespoons Parmesan cheese
1/2 teaspoon baking powder
1/2 teaspoon sugar
1 1/3 cups water
Vegetable cooking spray

Combine all ingredients in a large mixing bowl. Knead for five minutes, adding more water if needed to make a stiff but workable dough. Break off into large "meatball" sized balls. Flatten into patty shapes about 3 inches in diameter. Spray both sides with vegetable cooking spray and cook one side in a non stick skillet over medium heat for two minutes. Remove to counter, invert and, using a teaspoon, scoop a shallow depression out of the center. Then pinch up the sides to make a small border and return the sope to the skillet to continue cooking. After two minutes, invert once more so that the hollowed side is down. Cook one minute.

Top with black beans, low fat cheddar cheese, lettuce, Mock Sour Cream, Guacamole Surprise (from Spa Specialties), pico de gallo, picante sauce and pickled purple onion rings.

Yield: 12 servings

260 calories / 4.5 grams fat per serving

BLACK BEAN TAMALE PIE

This is an updated version of the traditional "tamal" which dates back to the Aztecs. Originally it was wrapped in banana leaves and baked, buried under ground. A non vegetarian version might include shredded, cooked chicken, pork and dried fruits.

2 cups frozen corn, thawed
1 cup chicken or vegetable stock
1 cup masa harina (available in the flour section in most grocery stores)
16 ounces creamed corn
1 teaspoon baking powder
2 tablespoons margarine, melted
4 ounces low fat cheddar cheese, grated
4 cups black beans, cooked and drained
1 teaspoon cumin
2 teaspoons chili powder
1/3 teaspoon garlic powder
1/3 teaspoon cayenne pepper
1/3 teaspoon oregano
1/4 cup tomato puree
1/2 cup green chiles, diced
Vegetable cooking spray

Puree corn briefly in a food processor. Combine in a bowl with stock, masa, creamed corn, baking powder and margarine.

Spray a baking dish with vegetable spray. Combine black beans with tomato puree and seasonings. Spread two-thirds of the masa-corn mixture in the bottom of the pan. Layer in the beans and cheese.

Top with the remaining masa-corn mixture, cover with foil and bake in a 350 degree oven. After 30 minutes, lower temperature to 300 degrees and bake one hour or until top is set. Serve with red and green salsas.

Yield: 6 servings

250 calories / 7 grams fat per serving

CHILE RELLENOS

Visually striking, with the dark green chile nestled in a robust red sauce; and absolutely delicious, with the mild cheese and sweetness of the raisins providing a perfect counterpoint to the piquancy of the pepper. Serve simply, with black beans, freshly made corn tortillas and Mexican beer for a meal to be remembered. And repeated.

4 large poblano chiles
4 ounces cooked rice
4 ounces lowfat cheddar cheese, shredded
2 tablespoons golden raisins
1 tablespoon chopped cilantro
vegetable cooking spray

Roast the chiles over an open flame until blackened. Dip into ice water, then peel off outer skin. Carefully slit down one side and remove the seeds.

Combine all other ingredients and use to stuff the chiles. Arrange the stuffed chiles on a baking pan sprayed with the vegetable spray.

Bake chiles for 10 to 15 minutes at 400 degrees until cheese melts. Serve with Roasted Red Pepper Salsa on page 80, in a wide soup bowl.

Yield: 4 servings

145 calories / 5.2 grams fat per serving

SPINACH FILLED CORN CREPES WITH A SMOKED TOMATO SAUCE

Who says enchiladas can't be elegant? Also try these with the crabmeat quesadilla filling given elsewhere in this book.

1/4 cup flour
1/4 cup stone ground cornmeal
1/2 cup masa harina (Quaker brand)
1 cup skim milk
1 egg, beaten
Vegetable cooking spray

Combine the first four ingredients into a smooth batter (You may add a few minced chives).

Spray a non stick skillet lightly with vegetable spray and ladle in just enough batter to cover the bottom. Cook over medium heat until the surface looks dry, then pry up one edge, flip the crepe and cook 30 seconds. Repeat.

The Filling:
12 ounces fresh spinach, cleaned and stemmed
1 cup sliced mushrooms
Vegetable cooking spray
2 tablespoons low fat cheddar
2 tablespoons Parmesan cheese

Steam spinach and squeeze out all moisture.

Saute mushrooms with vegetable spray. Combine spinach and mushrooms with remaining ingredients and use to fill crepes. Serve with the smoked tomato sauce.

SMOKED TOMATO SAUCE:
4 tomatoes
1 red bell pepper
1 onion
2 cloves garlic
1 tablespoon cilantro
1 cup tomato juice

Smoke tomatoes, red bell pepper and onion in a barbecue smoker for one hour. Puree with garlic, cilantro and tomato juice. Serve under filled crepes.

Yield: 4 servings
173 calories / 5.4 grams fat per serving

EGGPLANT ENCHILADAS

This recipe, one of our all time favorites, originally ran in Spa
Specialties, but without the Roasted Red Pepper Sauce, so we are
repeating it here for you. The sauce recipe is on page 80 .

Vegetable cooking spray
1 cup chopped onion
2 cloves garlic, minced
1/4 cup defatted chicken broth
1 teaspoon Worcestershire sauce
6 cups peeled, cubed eggplant (2 small)
1 cup chopped green pepper
1 cup sliced fresh mushrooms
2 tablespoons chopped, toasted almonds
1 teaspoon freshly ground black pepper
1 cup grated low fat Monterrey Jack cheese
1 tablespoon minced fresh parsley
12 whole wheat flour tortillas
Stock for softening tortillas

Saute onion and garlic in stock in a large skillet. Cook five minutes, then
stir in eggplant, green pepper, mushrooms and Worcestershire sauce.

Cook 10-12 minutes or until eggplant is soft. Remove from heat; add
almonds, parsley, pepper and 3/4 cup cheese.

Simmer a small amount of stock in a small frying pan. Dip tortillas in
individually on each side to soften. Place a portion of the eggplant mix in
each tortilla and roll tightly. Place seam side down in a glass baking dish
sprayed with vegetable spray. Top with remaining cheese and bake 20
minutes at 350 degrees.

Yield: 12 servings (one enchilada each)

168 calories / 5.4 grams fat per enchilada
Contributed by Trisha Shirey

MUSHROOMS STROGANOFF

Serve with a bright green vegetable for a light, completely vegetarian supper. And for some reason, this dish tastes even better if you can play a little Viennese waltz music in the background during the preparation. (Dancing in the kitchen is permitted.)

1 small onion, coarsely chopped
2 cloves garlic, minced
2 tablespoons margarine
1 1/2 pounds mushrooms, thinly sliced
2 tablespoons flour
1 cup water
1 vegetable broth cube
1 tablespoon tomato paste
1 tablespoon fresh tarragon, minced, or Mexican marigold mint
1/2 cup light or nonfat sour cream
2 tablespoons white wine
12 ounces linguine, cooked al dente
Freshly ground black pepper

Saute the onion and garlic over medium heat in the margarine until softened but not browned. Add the mushrooms and saute for a few more minutes.

Stir in the flour and cook, stirring for one minute. Whisk in the water, stirring, and bring to a simmer. Add the vegetable cube, tomato paste and white wine. Simmer for ten minutes. Add the tarragon.

Heat the linguine. Just before serving, add sour cream to the mushroom mixture and heat through (do not boil or the sauce will separate) and pour over pasta. Grate pepper over all.

Yield: 4 servings

290 calories / 6.2 grams fat per serving

PINTO BEAN PIE WITH CORN TOPPING

The thinking man's version of the ubiquitous "Frito Pie". Feel free to add sliced jalapeños anywhere along the line.

4 cups cooked pinto beans (with some of the cooking liquid reserved)
1/4 cup chili powder
1 tablespoon cumin powder
1/2 cup tomato puree
1/4 cup corn masa

Combine seasonings, tomato puree and masa. Blend into beans and cook until slightly thickened. Remove from heat. Add the following:

2 cups pico de gallo (page 76)
1/2 cup diced green chiles

Spoon the mixture into individual ramekins. Top with the corn topping and bake.

The Topping:
3 tablespoons margarine
3 cups frozen corn, thawed
2 teaspoons sugar
1/2 teaspoon salt
2 eggs
1 egg white
Paprika

Puree the corn. In a heavy saucepan, melt margarine, stir in corn, sugar and salt.

Beat eggs and whites together.

Over very low heat, incorporate eggs into corn mixture a little at a time, stirring until thickened, about 10 minutes. Spread mixture over individual casseroles, sprinkle with paprika and bake at 350 degrees until the top is set, about 45 minutes.

Serve with your favorite salsa.

Yield: 8 servings

282 calories / 6.5 grams fat per serving

BAKED POLENTA AND CHEESE

We usually think of polenta as an Italian dish, but I'm near certain American Indians were concocting similar fare long before Mrs. Columbus' wandering boy ever set sail.

4 cups water
1 red bell pepper, finely diced
1 yellow bell pepper, finely diced
1 poblano pepper, finely diced
3/4 cup cilantro, chopped
1/2 teaspoon salt
1/2 teaspoon black pepper
1 tablespoon chili powder
2 cups coarse cornmeal
6 ounces low fat cheddar (6 one-ounce pieces)
Vegetable cooking spray

Bring water to a boil with peppers, cilantro, salt and pepper.

Stir in cornmeal. Reduce heat to low; cook 15 minutes, stirring often. (Don't scorch).

Spray six ramekins with the vegetable spray; fill with polenta.

Insert a piece of cheese into each. Chill until firm, about thirty minutes. Remove from ramekin by running a knife around the edge and then inverting.

Bake on sprayed baking sheet at 350 degrees for 10 minutes.

Serve with the Roasted Red Pepper Sauce on page 80 .

Yield: 6 servings

173 calories / 5.2 grams fat per serving

CHEESE POLENTA

This is a more traditional, but equally delicious, version of polenta using grits and incorporating cheese into the batter. Take any leftovers, crisp them up in a skillet with some vegetable spray and serve them for breakfast with some warm maple syrup. Really!

1 cup corn grits
3-1/2 cups boiling water
1 egg, beaten
2 ounces low fat cheddar
2 ounces Parmesan cheese
1 teaspoon garlic powder
1/4 teaspoon cayenne pepper
1 tablespoon margarine
Vegetable cooking spray

Stir grits into boiling water and cook, stirring occasionally until thickened; 5-7 minutes. Mix a little of this mixture with the egg and then pour all ingredients into the grits mixture and continue to cook for about one minute.

Spray a 8 x 8 inch baking pan with vegetable spray, pour in grits and bake at 350 degrees for 45 minutes or until firm and slightly crusted on top. May be served at this point, if desired. Or, refrigerate overnight then cut into squares and grill or saute with vegetable spray until crisp and warm. Serve with Roasted Pepper Sauce or Salsa Verde (recipes in "Sauces" section).

Yield: 4 servings

173 calories / 6 grams fat per serving

SPINACH LASAGNA

A Lake Austin classic. Double the recipe and freeze individual portions for a quick lunch or easy dinner. It's not necessary to cook the noodles first. They are easier to work with uncooked and it saves time too.

The Sauce:
1 onion, chopped
1 tablespoon olive oil
10 cloves garlic, minced
3 cups mushrooms, sliced
2 bay leaves
1 tablespoon oregano
1 1/2 tablespoons basil
1/4 cup parsley, chopped
3 cups diced tomatoes, fresh or canned
3 cups tomato sauce
1 teaspoon freshly ground black pepper
1/8 teaspoon salt
1/8 teaspoon sugar

Saute the onion in olive oil until clear. Add the garlic and mushrooms and saute for five more minutes. Add remaining ingredients and simmer for thirty minutes.

Vegetable cooking spray
1 10 ounce package frozen spinach, thawed
1 cup egg whites (8 large eggs)
2 cups part skim ricotta cheese
8 ounces whole wheat lasagna noodles, uncooked
8 ounces part skim mozzarella cheese, thinly sliced
1/4 cup grated parmesan

Spray a 9 x 13 baking pan with vegetable spray.

Place the spinach in cheesecloth or a kitchen towel and squeeze all the liquid from the spinach. Set aside.

Place the egg whites in a mixer bowl and whip on high for one minute. Add the ricotta and whip for two more minutes.

Spread a thin layer of the sauce on the bottom of the pan. Place one layer of noodles on the sauce. Spread more sauce on top of the noodles. Place half of the spinach evenly over the sauce. Distribute half of the ricotta mix evenly. Then spread one layer of half of the mozzarella. Layer more noodles and repeat the process, ending with a layer of noodles, tomato sauce and remaining mozzarella.

For a neater finished casserole, firmly press the lasagna noodles in place in each layer.

Bake covered for 30 minutes at 375 degrees. Uncover and bake until browned and bubbling, about fifteen minutes.

Allow to stand for fifteen minutes before slicing and serving. Sprinkle with parmesan cheese before serving.

Yield: 8 servings

307 calories / 9.2 grams fat per serving

Thanks to Mike Conner and Shirley Mixen for their input on this recipe.

MEATLESS MUFFALETTA

This vegetarian version of a New Orleans classic is the sort of lip smackin', finger lickin', down in the trenches stuff guaranteed to please even the most devoted carnivore. Set this out at half time and watch it get pounced on like a fumble at the five yard line.

6 - 1/4 inch slices of eggplant
2 sliced tomatoes, liquid pressed out using a paper towel
5 ounce jar olive salad, drained
5 ounce jar mixed pepper salad, drained
1/4 cup pickled hot cherry peppers, drained and sliced
1 tablespoon olive oil
1 tablespoon balsamic or red wine vinegar
1 tablespoon fresh oregano, chopped or 1/2 tablespoon dry
1 clove garlic, minced
1 large round sourdough loaf (7")
6 ounces smoked mozzarella or low fat provolone, sliced
vegetable cooking spray

Saute the eggplant briefly with vegetable spray.

Combine first nine ingredients, let stand 30 minutes.

Slice the top inch off of the bread loaf and hollow out the inside, leaving a one inch thickness of crust. Add 2/3 of the pickled mix to bottom bread piece. Top with cheese and then the remaining mix.

Weight down with a plate and a heavy skillet for 30 minutes.

Cut into wedges and serve.

Yield: 6 servings

286 calories / 5.5 grams fat per serving

To reduce sodium, rinse the olives and peppers well, then drain well.

RED BEAN CHILI WITH GRILLED POLENTA CROUTONS

This hearty vegetarian chili is for all those leather bustin', trail ridin', dogie ropin' buckaroos in your family. When they ask you what those things on the top are, don't tell them they're "polenta croutons". Tell 'em they're cow chips. They'll love you for it. Pardner.

The Croutons:
1 1/2 cups yellow cornmeal
1 cup cold water
1 cup boiling water
1/4 teaspoon salt
1/4 cup Parmesan cheese

Mix cornmeal with cold water. Add to boiling water. Cook, stirring over low heat until thickened; about 5 minutes. Add salt and cheese.

Spread onto a sheet pan and refrigerate overnight. Cut into 2" squares and grill or saute' in a nonstick skillet with vegetable spray until crispy on the outside. Cut into smaller squares and use to top chili.

The Chili:
1 tablespoon olive oil
1/4 onion, diced
4 cloves garlic, minced
16 ounces tomatoes, diced
2 tablespoons tomato paste
1/4 cup chili powder
1 teaspoon oregano
2 teaspoons cumin
6 cups red beans, cooked
Pinch of cayenne pepper
1 ounce grated low fat cheddar cheese

Saute onions and garlic in oil. Add the tomato paste and seasonings. Add beans and simmer for 20 minutes. Serve in a large bowl topped with croutons and grated cheddar cheese.

Yield: 12 servings

225 calories / 3.2 grams fat per 1 1/4 cup serving

SUMMER SQUASH TORTA

Proof that a quesadilla by any other name would taste as sweet. This has become one of the most popular and widely requested recipes at the resort, deservedly so. Serve it with black beans and a fruit salad. (If this dish is served as a leftover, it becomes known as a "re-torta".)

1 large zucchini, cut in half across, then sliced lengthwise
1 large yellow squash, cut in half across, then sliced lengthwise
1/2 red bell pepper, sliced into thin rings

Steam all vegetables together until just tender.

2 ounces low fat cheddar cheese, grated
2 ounces low fat cottage cheese
2 tablespoons Parmesan cheese
1 teaspoon cumin
2 cloves garlic, minced
1 serrano pepper, seeded and minced (optional)

Blend all ingredients together.

2 whole wheat flour tortillas
Vegetable cooking spray

Spread cheese mixture on one tortilla. Top with vegetables and cover with other tortilla.

Spray a nonstick skillet with vegetable spray. Slide in the torta, cover and cook over medium heat for a few minutes. Remove torta from the skillet, re-spray, invert torta, slide it back into the skillet, cover and cook until cheese is melted and tortillas are browned. Cut into quarters and serve with Salsa Verde and a dollop of Mock Sour Cream. (Recipes in Sauces section.)

Yield: 4 servings

190 calories / 6.5 grams fat per serving

PASTA WITH LEMON PARSLEY DRESSING

A simple but absolutely delicious salad.

1/2 cup packed fresh parsley, finely chopped
2 large garlic cloves, minced
1/2 teaspoon lemon zest, minced
1 tablespoon olive oil, divided
1 twelve ounce can Italian plum tomatoes, chopped (reserve liquid)
1 tablespoon minced fresh basil
2 cups hot cooked pasta (Penne, rotini or bows)

Combine parsley, lemon zest and garlic and set aside.

Heat 1/2 tablespoon of the olive oil and add tomatoes. Bring to a boil and cook ten minutes. Add the basil to the tomatoes.

Toss the pasta with the remaining oil. Add the parsley mixture and the tomatoes and mix gently. Serve warm. Top with grated Parmesan if desired.

Yield: 4 servings

144 calories / 3.9 grams fat per serving

SPANISH POTATO TORTE

This versatile dish can be served either warm or at room temperature and makes a great Sunday brunch entree, a nifty light lunch any day or, cut into smaller wedges, a tasty "tapa" or appetizer.

5 medium potatoes, peeled and thinly sliced
Olive flavored cooking spray
1 small onion, halved and thinly sliced
2 eggs
2 egg whites
Pinch of salt
Black pepper

Preheat oven to 350 degrees. Toss potatoes with cooking spray in a small roasting pan. Cover and bake for 20 minutes.

Add onion, cover and bake ten minutes or until done. Let cool.

Beat eggs and whites with salt and pepper. Fold in potato-onion mixture.

Coat a large saute pan with olive flavored spray. Heat to high, pour in potato and egg mixture, shake to settle vegetables, lower heat to lowest possible setting and cook 15 minutes or until mostly set.

Place large plate on skillet and deftly invert. Slide inverted torte back into skillet to finish. Cut into wedges and serve with the pepper sauce on the next page

PEPPER SAUCE:

1/2 teaspoon chili powder
1/4 teaspoon cayenne pepper
2 cloves garlic
2 tablespoons sliced and toasted almonds
1 tablespoon olive oil
2 red bell peppers, roasted, peeled and seeded (see Glossary)
2 tablespoons red wine vinegar

Combine and puree all ingredients.

Yield: 8 servings

156 calories / 4.5 grams fat per serving

VEGETABLE PAELLA

Saffron is the handpicked pistil from a Spanish poppy. Scarcity and the nature of the work make it the world's most expensive spice, but fortunately, a little goes a long way.

2 teaspoons olive oil, divided
2 tablespoons minced onion
2 cloves garlic, minced
1 cup long grain rice
2 1/2 cups chicken stock, divided
1/2 teaspoon saffron threads
1 small zucchini, cut into 3/4-inch chunks
1 small red bell pepper, coarsely diced
2 mushrooms, quartered
1/2 small onion, coarsely diced
4 slices of eggplant, sliced 1/2-inch thick and quartered
4 artichoke hearts, rinsed and halved
4 black olives, sliced
1 large tomato, cut into 8 wedges
1/4 cup frozen green peas, defrosted
Chives

Saute onion and garlic in one teaspoon oil until slightly softened; add rice for one minute.

Pour in 1-1/2 cups chicken stock and saffron. Cover tightly and cook until dry but not mushy; 20 minutes.

Steam zucchini, red pepper, onion, mushrooms, and eggplant until almost tender.

Saute all vegetables along with artichokes, black olives, tomato and peas in one teaspoon of oil for two minutes.

Mold rice into four large, flat soup bowls; surround with vegetables and pour 1/4 cup broth in each bowl. Garnish with chives.

Yield: 4 servings
165 calories / 2.2 grams fat per serving

VEGETABLE TORTINI

A sturdy, 'stick to the ribs' casserole, suitable for either a vegetarian entree or a substantial side dish.

1 medium eggplant, sliced lengthwise, 1/4-inch thick
6 slices whole wheat bread
3 medium baking potatoes, sliced lengthwise, 1/4-inch thick
2 teaspoons dried basil or 1 1/2 tablespoons fresh
1 tablespoon minced fresh parsley
1 teaspoon black pepper
8 ounces part skim mozzarella cheese, grated
12 egg whites
4 medium zucchini, sliced lengthwise 1/4-inch thick
2 cups canned tomatoes, drained and diced
Vegetable cooking spray

Cut the eggplant, salt lightly and place on a towel to allow to "sweat". (This helps extract any possible bitterness.) Rinse and pat dry.

Steam or microwave the potatoes until tender.

Place the bread slices in a food processor and use the metal blade to process until they are soft bread crumbs. Mix the herbs and spices with the bread crumbs.

Coat the bottom and sides of a 9 x 13-inch baking dish with vegetable cooking spray. Coat the pan heavily with 1/3 of the crumbs and press firmly. Place the eggplant slices in a single layer over the bread crumbs and sprinkle them with 1/2 of the cheese. Place the potato slices in a single layer over the cheese and sprinkle with 1/3 of the bread crumbs. Then cover the bread crumbs with the remaining cheese. Top with the remaining egg whites. Add a single layer of zucchini. Spread the canned tomatoes over the squash and sprinkle with the remaining bread crumbs. Bake at 325 degrees for 50 minutes.

Yield: 12 servings (141 calories / 5 grams fat per serving)

Contributed by Mike Conner

VEGETARIAN POT PIE

A revamped recipe from the sixties when the choice of herbs might have been a little more 'eclectic'. This one you can and will inhale.

The vegetables:
1 large potato, peeled, diced
2 carrots, peeled and diced
1 small turnip, peeled and diced
1/2 onion, diced
1 rib celery, diced
1/4 green peas
1/4 corn kernels
1/4 cup lima beans
4 green beans, cut into pieces

Steam vegetables until carrots are <u>just</u> done. Feel free to make any vegetable substitutions your garden or refrigerator may offer.

The sauce:
12 ounces evaporated skim milk
3 tablespoons white wine
1 tablespoon cornstarch
1/4 teaspoon white pepper
1/8 teaspoon nutmeg
3 tablespoons reduced fat cream cheese
1/4 cup Parmesan cheese
2 tablespoons minced fresh herbs (any combination of oregano, thyme, rosemary, marjoram, parsley, chives, etc.) or 1 tablespoon dried

Bring the milk to a simmer in a medium saucepan. Mix wine and cornstarch together then whisk into milk. Return to simmer, add remaining ingredients, stirring until smooth. Combine the sauce with the vegetables, then ladle into four ovenproof soup crocks.

The topping:
A three sheet thickness of phyllo pastry
vegetable cooking spray

Lay the stacked sheets out on a flat surface. Spray with vegetable spray. Fold in half, spray again. Fold in half again and spray. With a sharp knife, cut into four equal pieces and top each pot pie, tucking the edges of the phyllo under the inside lip of the crocks.

Bake at 400 degrees until slightly browned and crispy.

Yield: 4 servings

175 calories / 2.5 grams fat per serving

WILD MUSHROOM RAVIOLI WITH BASIL CREAM

Simple, yet sophisticated. These silken ravioli spun from wonton wrappers are worthy of your best china.

1 pound wild mushrooms, sliced (shitake, chanterelle, porto bello or a mix)
1 leek, cleaned and minced (white with a little green)
2 cloves garlic, minced
1 teaspoon margarine
Vegetable cooking spray
3 ounces low fat cream cheese, softened
1 teaspoon lemon juice
Freshly ground black pepper
1/8 teaspoon cayenne pepper

Saute mushrooms, leek and garlic in margarine and vegetable spray until softened.

Blend the cream cheese, lemon juice and peppers. Combine with the mushroom mixture.

Cornstarch
Won ton wrappers
Egg white

Line a baking sheet with wax paper. Sprinkle with cornstarch. Fill won tons with mushroom mix, fold over into triangles and brush the edges with egg white to seal. Store on baking sheet covered with plastic.

To cook, drop wontons into a large pot of boiling water for three minutes. Remove with a slotted spoon, and drain well. Serve with Basil Cream Sauce, page 60.

Yield: 6 servings

215 calories / 3 grams fat per serving

Beef and Pork Entrees

ENCHILADAS DE RES

These lean, spicy enchiladas are a big step above what you get in most Tex-Mex restaurants and actually much more like what you might expect to find in the interior of Mexico.

Filling:
1 pound Carabeef* (or very lean ground beef)
3/4 cup onion, diced
1 clove garlic, minced
1 small zucchini, finely diced
1 small carrot, peeled and finely diced
3/4 cup potato, peeled and finely diced
2 large tomatoes, peeled, seeded and pureed
1 tablespoon parsley
1/4 teaspoon cinnamon
1/8 teaspoon clove
2 cups low-sodium beef stock
12 corn tortillas

Saute the beef with onion and garlic over medium heat until cooked through. Add zucchini, carrot and potato along with enough beef stock to cover. Simmer until vegetables are just tender, then drain, reserving the liquid. Return meat to skillet, add tomato, parsley and spices. Cook until almost dry. Steam tortillas briefly to soften. Fill with meat mixture, roll up and place in baking dish.

Sauce:
2 cups reserved beef broth
1/2 cup canned tomato puree
3 tablespoons chili powder
2 teaspoons cumin
1/2 teaspoon garlic powder

Simmer all ingredients together in a saucepan over medium heat until reduced to a sauce-like consistency. Pour over enchiladas. Bake in a preheated 400 degree oven for 15 minutes.

Garnish with a little shredded lettuce, thinly sliced radish, minced onion and sliced pickled jalapeño all tossed in a bit of vinegar and olive oil.

Yield: 6 servings

322 calories / 5.4 grams fat per serving

*Carabeef is the trade name for water buffalo meat, which is lower in fat than skinless chicken breast. It is available in some natural food stores.

STUFFED PORK TENDERLOIN WITH BLACKBERRY SAUCE

We like to think we always give our chefs enough leeway to be creative and occasionally they reward us by coming back with dishes as good as this.

1 12-ounce pork tenderloin, trimmed
1/2 cup cooked wild rice
1 tablespoon diced red bell pepper
1 tablespoon diced yellow bell pepper
1 tablespoon diced green bell pepper
1 egg white
1/4 cup diced onion
1 teaspoon garlic, minced
48 inches cotton string
Dash black pepper
Dash marjoram
1 tablespoon honey

Sauce:
1 cup blackberries, pureed
1/4 cup rich stock
1 tablespoon Brandy or Madeira wine
1 dash garlic powder
1 tablespoon sugar
1 tablespoon raspberry vinegar
1 tablespoon cornstarch
1 tablespoon cold water

Butterfly the pork loin, and set aside.

Combine the peppers, rice and egg white. Saute the onion and garlic until onion is clear, add to pepper and rice mixture.

Cut the string into 6-inch pieces and spread evenly one inch apart. Lay tenderloin, open faced, horizontally across the string. Fill center of loin with stuffing. Starting at one end, tie the ends of the butterflied tenderloin together.

Place the tenderloin in a baking pan, cover with pepper and marjoram, brush with honey and bake covered at 300 degrees for about 45 minutes or until internal temperature reaches 160 degrees.

Puree blackberries until smooth. Strain out seeds. Put pureed berries in a saucepan on low flame. Add stock, brandy and garlic powder.

Over high heat, caramelize sugar in vinegar and add to sauce. Combine cold water and cornstarch, add to sauce and bring to a boil.

Serve tenderloin slices in a bed of blackberry sauce.

Yield: 4 servings

280 calories / 4.1 grams fat per serving

Contributed by Michael Conner

GREEN CHILE STEW

After a tough day of tramping about in the winter cold, nothing quite fills the bill like a big steaming bowl of stew, salad and some freshly made corn tortillas or cornbread. Serve an apple currant cobbler (page 253) for dessert.

2 pounds Carabeef* round roast, cut into 1/2-inch cubes
2 tablespoons olive oil
1 small onion, diced
4 small potatoes, peeled and diced
4 zucchini, cubed
12 green chiles, roasted, peeled and diced or 8 ounces canned chiles
4 cloves garlic, minced
6 cups beef stock, chicken stock or a combination
2 tablespoons cilantro, chopped

Brown the meat in oil, then the onions. De-glaze the pan with the stock, scraping the bottom well. Reintroduce the beef and simmer (approximately 1 1/2 hours) until almost tender. Add garlic, potatoes, zucchini and chiles and simmer until potatoes are done. Garnish with chopped cilantro.

Yield: 8 servings

246 calories / 5.4 grams fat per serving

* Carabeef is the trade name for naturally raised water buffalo meat which is leaner than chicken breast. It is available in many fine restaurants and health food stores. The company is located in Arkansas.

OVEN BEEF AND VEGETABLE STEW

Try substituting two cups (plus one glass) of dry red wine in place of two cups of the beef stock for an interesting twist. Serve simply, with a green salad and some good French bread. (The two cups are for the stew, the glass is for the cook.)

1 1/2 pounds Carabeef* rump, cubed
1/4 cup flour
6 small onions
2 potatoes, peeled and cut into chunks
3 carrots, cut into chunks
6 mushroom caps
3 cloves garlic, minced
2 cups turnips, diced
4 cups beef stock
8 ounces tomato sauce
1 teaspoon dried thyme
1/2 teaspoon dried oregano
1/4 teaspoon black pepper
1 bay leaf
1/2 teaspoon orange zest, grated

Toss beef with flour. Combine with other ingredients. Bake, covered at 325 degrees for three hours, stirring occasionally.

Yield: 8 servings

240 calories / 4.2 grams fat per serving

* Carabeef is the trade name for naturally raised water buffalo meat which can be found in fine restaurants and health food stores. The meat is leaner than chicken breast.

MIXED VEGETABLE, BEAN, SAUSAGE STEW

If you like 'peasant style' dishes, try this one with its earthy, eclectic array of ingredients and subtly exotic seasonings.

1 cup chick peas, soaked overnight, drained
1 cup great northern beans, soaked overnight, drained
1 bunch Swiss chard, leaves sliced into 1/2-inch strips, stalks unstrung and
    chopped
3 quarts mixture chicken/beef stock
2 stalks celery, unstrung and chopped
6 cloves garlic, minced
1 bay leaf
1 tablespoon paprika
1/4 teaspoon cumin
1/4 teaspoon cloves
1/4 teaspoon nutmeg
Freshly ground black pepper
1/2 teaspoon red pepper flakes
2 teaspoons salt
5 carrots, cut into bite-size pieces
1/2 pound butternut squash, peeled, in bite-size pieces
3 small potatoes, peeled in bite-size pieces
2 pounds Carabeef* sausage, cut into bite-size chunks
12 ounces nitrate-free ham, cut into small cubes
Chopped parsley for garnish

Simmer chick peas in stock for 30 minutes.

Add beans, simmer 30 minutes. Add chard stalks, celery, seasonings and sausage and simmer for 45 minutes. Add remaining ingredients, simmer until vegetables are done.

Yield: 12 servings
256 calories / 4.5 grams fat per serving

*Carabeef is the trade name for naturally raised water buffalo. See
 Glossary

TACO SALAD

You can't live in Texas and not love tacos. We eat them soft or crispy, made with flour or corn tortillas; we fill them with eggs, with beans, with meat and vegetables; and we douse them with salsas - red, green, or in between. We even serve them as salads!

1 pound ground Carabeef*
1/4 cup minced onion
1 clove minced garlic
1/4 teaspoon oregano
1 teaspoon cumin
1 tablespoon chili powder
Water
12 corn tortillas, quartered and baked (see recipe page 35)
4 cups cooked pinto beans, warmed
2 or 3 tomatoes, diced
1 onion, diced
8 cups shredded lettuce
1/2 cup grated low fat cheddar
Salsa (see recipes in the Sauces section)

Saute the Carabeef in a non stick skillet until it begins to gray. Add the onion, the garlic and seasonings and cook until vegetables are slightly softened.

Add water to cover and simmer until water is evaporated.

Ladle 1/2 cup beans onto each of 8 large plates. Top with 2 ounces of Carabeef, garnish all with vegetables and cheese. Surround with tortilla chips and serve with bowls of salsa and plenty of napkins!

Yield: 8 servings (345 calories / 3.8 grams fat per serving)

* Carabeef is the trade name for lean, naturally raised water buffalo. See the glossary for more information.

Chicken

APPLE GLAZED CHICKEN
WITH HORSERADISH CREAM

This dish may be baked (especially if you are preparing in quantity) to equally good effect. Simply place the chicken breasts into a sprayed baking pan, top each with a slice of apple and then the glaze. Bake at 400 degrees for 15 - 20 minutes. Top with horseradish cream and maybe a sprinkle of minced chives for a festive, winter holiday look.

4 boneless skinless chicken breasts
1-1/2 cups apple cider
Juice from one lime
1 tablespoon honey
1 tablespoon cider vinegar
1/2 teaspoon minced rosemary

Marinate chicken breasts in the above mixture for 2-6 hours. Remove chicken and reduce the marinade to a syrupy consistency in a saucepan over medium high heat. Grill chicken, basting with glaze. Take

1 Macintosh apple, cored and sliced

Grill until slightly softened. Serve chicken and apple slices with the following sauce.

Sauce:
1/4 cup fat free mayonnaise
1/4 cup applesauce
2 teaspoons horseradish
1/4 teaspoon balsamic vinegar.

Combine sauce ingredients and chill.

Yield: 4 servings

196 calories / 4.5 grams fat per serving

ATHENIAN CHICKEN

This dish has more assembly steps than a new Ford truck, but don't be daunted; most of them can be done ahead of time, and the finished result is well worth the effort involved.

4 four ounce chicken breasts, pounded out to 1/4" thickness
Olive oil flavored non stick spray
4 teaspoons golden raisins
2 tablespoons Madeira wine
2 ounces ricotta cheese
1 ounce nitrate free ham, slivered
4 teaspoons pinenuts
1 clove garlic, minced
2 tablespoons minced fresh basil
Pinch of cayenne

Soak the raisins in the Madeira wine for fifteen minutes.

Combine all ingredients and divide evenly among the four chicken breasts, placing the mixture in the center of each breast. Roll up the chicken breasts tightly and secure with toothpicks.

Brown the chicken breasts in a skillet sprayed with olive oil flavored non stick spray.

Add to the chicken:
1 tablespoon lemon juice
3 tablespoons chicken stock

Cover, and let chicken finish cooking over low heat, turning occasionally. Set chicken aside, but keep warm.

Sauce:
Juice of 1/2 lemon
1 cup chicken stock
1/4 teaspoon julienned lemon zest
1/2 teaspoon cornstarch

Combine in a small saucepan and cook over medium heat, stirring until slightly thickened. Set aside.

Spinach Base:
2 cups tightly packed, washed and trimmed fresh spinach
1/4 cup thinly sliced fresh mushrooms
1 clove garlic, minced
Vegetable cooking spray
2 tablespoons freshly grated Parmesan cheese

Saute the mushrooms and garlic with non stick spray over medium heat until softened, increase heat, toss in spinach and, stirring constantly, cook down until wilted.

Divide this mixture over four plates. Remove toothpicks, slice the chicken breasts into 1/2 inch thick slices and arrange over the spinach. Drizzle with the lemon sauce and dust with parmesan cheese.

Yield: 4 servings

285 calories / 5.6 grams fat per serving

AZTEC CHICKEN

Achiote are the orange-red seeds of the tropical annatto tree. They have been used to season and color pork, beef, chicken, beans and rice for centuries. Look for them in your herb market, Mexican grocery or health food store. You may also find a paste form called achiotina or achioto condimentado. Substitute half the amount of paste for seeds.

Hoja santa is a native of Mexico which is commonly found around streams and river beds. The large leaves have a faintly licorice or sasparilla flavor. A large (to six feet) attractive plant, it has a rather rambunctious growth habit, a lot like bamboo. The leaves are often used as tamale wrappers or to wrap fish or meat for grilling. Banana leaves could be used for a substitute and discarded after grilling.

1/3 cup achiote (annatto seeds)
Water to cover

Simmer the achiote in water for about ten minutes until almost all liquid has evaporated. Allow to sit and soften. Crush the seeds in a mortar before grinding along with the following, into a paste.

1 teaspoon cumin
1 teaspoon oregano
10 peppercorns
1/2 teaspoon allspice
6 cloves garlic, peeled
1 teaspoon salt
1/2 cup orange juice
1/2 cup grapefruit juice
Juice of one lime

Now take 8 boneless, skinless chicken breasts. Prick them all over with a fork. Thin the achiote paste as needed with a little water, then spread all over chicken. Reserve some of the paste for topping. Allow to marinate overnight or at least six hours.

8 hoja santa leaves, lightly steamed

Remove chicken from marinade and discard the used marinade. Wrap chicken in leaves; grill over charcoal.

Top with sliced onion and tomato sauteed in a little olive oil and vegetable spray with some of the reserved seasoning paste.

Yield: 8 servings

230 calories / 4.5 grams fat per serving

BASIL AND ARTICHOKE CHICKEN

As an alternative try pearl onions, white wine and chicken stock in place of the leeks, red wine and beef stock, and discover the fair sister of this dark beauty. In either version, a good, sturdy stock and fresh basil are the keys to success.

Vegetable cooking spray
1 tablespoon olive oil
6 four ounce boneless, skinless chicken breasts
2 cloves garlic, minced
1/2 cup minced leeks (white part and a little of the green)
3/4 cup red wine
1 1/2 cups strong beef stock
3/4 cup chopped tomato
2 teaspoons minced fresh basil
9 canned artichoke hearts, drained, rinsed and halved
1/4 cup nitrate free ham, minced
2 teaspoons cornstarch mixed with 1/4 cup strong beef stock
Pinch of cayenne

Brown the chicken breasts in a skillet using the vegetable spray. Set aside.

In the same skillet, saute garlic, leeks and ham briefly in olive oil. Deglaze the pan with the red wine, scraping up any brown bits in the pan with a wooden spoon.

Return the chicken to the skillet along with stock, basil, tomato and cayenne. Cover and simmer until tender, approximately fifteen minutes. Remove the chicken to a serving platter and keep warm.

Add artichoke hearts to the skillet, thicken the sauce with the cornstarch mixture and pour over the chicken.

Yield: 6 servings

240 calories / 5.2 grams fat per serving

CHICKEN ENCHILADAS SUIZAS

Mexican food with manners. These will melt in your mouth <u>without</u> melting your mouth. We recommend that you not assemble the enchiladas until you are ready to cook them. Unsauced, the tortillas dry out, and sauced and sitting, they get soggy.

Suiza Sauce:
5 tomatoes, charred on a grill or under a broiler
1/2 large onion, chopped
1 clove garlic, minced
1 teaspoon vegetable oil
1 cup tomato juice
1 can evaporated skim milk
1 tablespoon cornstarch, mixed with a little of the skim milk

Combine all the vegetables in a food processor or blender and process until smooth. Saute this mixture in vegetable oil for ten minutes, stirring occasionally.

Add the tomato juice and simmer for ten minutes. Add one and one half cans of milk. Combine the remaining milk and cornstarch.
Add, but do not allow the sauce to boil. Cook until slightly thickened.

Per enchilada:
1 1/2 ounce poached chicken breast
1/4 ounce low fat cheddar
1/4 teaspoon canned green chiles
1 corn tortilla

Preheat the oven to 400 degrees.

Dip the tortillas in the warm suiza sauce. Fill with remaining ingredients and roll up.

Place the enchiladas in a baking dish and top with sauce. Add additional cheddar if desired.

Bake for ten minutes at 400 degrees. Garnish with mock sour cream if desired. (See page 72.)

Yield: 6 servings (2 enchiladas per person)

275 calories / 4 grams fat per serving

CHICKEN GUMBO

To some minds, this is not the most visually appealing dish we do, although I personally think it has a certain earthy appeal. In any case, even if you find yourself among it's visual critics, you will find that it tastes so good you will want to make it and eat it with your eyes closed.

Please refer to page 281 for a note of caution about making roux.

1 pound boneless, skinless chicken breasts, cut into bite sized pieces
1 tablespoon vegetable oil
1 tablespoon flour
1 serrano pepper, seeded and minced
1 cup diced onion
1/3 cup diced celery
1 cup diced green bell pepper
4 cloves garlic
1/3 cup minced parsley
1/2 cup brown rice
1/4 teaspoon ground coriander
1/4 teaspoon ground cumin
1/8 teaspoon cayenne
8 ounces okra, sliced
1 teaspoon gumbo file powder
1 quart defatted chicken stock
Non stick spray

Cook the oil and flour in a heavy skillet over medium heat, stirring constantly until the roux is a dark chocolate color.

Add the vegetables (except okra) and saute until well coated and slightly softened.

Bring stock to a simmer in a large pot and whisk in roux mixture.
Add rice, chicken, parsley and seasonings (except file). Simmer for thirty minutes.

In a non stick sprayed skillet, briefly saute the okra. Add to the gumbo and simmer for fifteen minutes.

Add the file and serve hot.

Yield: 6 servings

210 calories / 4.5 grams fat per serving

CHICKEN MILANESE

Accompany this crunchy chicken dish with a bright green vegetable and then finish with the Sicilian Orange Sorbet on page 270.

6 four ounce chicken breasts, cut in half, pounded out 1/4 " thick between two sheets of plastic wrap
2 egg whites, beaten with 3/4 cup buttermilk
2 cups fresh whole wheat bread crumbs
6 tablespoons Parmesan cheese
1/2 teaspoon garlic powder
1/2 teaspoon cayenne
Olive oil flavored non stick spray
2 teaspoons clarified margarine (see Glossary)

Preheat the oven to 375 degrees.

Combine the bread crumbs, parmesan and spices.

Dip the chicken into the egg wash, then press into the bread crumb mixture.

Spray both sides of the chicken with the olive oil spray; then saute in a non stick skillet in margarine until browned.

Top with the tomato basil sauce and serve.

Tomato Basil Sauce:
2 cups diced canned tomatoes
1/4 cup onion, diced
2 cloves garlic, minced
1 teaspoon olive oil
2 tablespoons tomato paste
Pinch cayenne
2 tablespoons chopped fresh basil

Saute onion and garlic in the olive oil. Add the tomatoes, paste and cayenne.

Simmer to desired consistency. Puree in blender or food processor then strain through a sieve.

Add the basil, reheat.

Yield: 6 servings

284 calories / 6.3 grams fat per serving

CHICKEN IN RASPBERRY VINEGAR

This is one of the most popular dishes served at Lake Austin Spa Resort and in a sense, epitomizes everything we are trying to accomplish in our nutrition programs. It is lean, nutritious, easy to prepare, slightly unusual, and has both great taste and visual appeal.

The vinegar that we use is made by Trisha Shirey, our grounds manager. Raspberry, blackberry, blueberry, strawberry and other flavored vinegars are available from "Natural Expressions", the Lake Austin Spa Resort shop.

4 chicken breasts, boneless and skinless
1/2 cup raspberry vinegar (or other fruit vinegar)
1/4 cup beef or chicken stock
1/4 cup minced shallots
1 teaspoon cornstarch, dissolved in 1 tablespoon beef or chicken stock
1 teaspoon unsweetened frozen raspberry juice concentrate
Freshly ground black pepper (to taste)
1/4 cup fresh or thawed frozen raspberries
Vegetable cooking spray

Brown the chicken breasts in a non stick skillet that has been sprayed with vegetable spray. Cook over medium heat until browned on both sides. Lower heat, cover and cook chicken until done. Remove chicken from the pan, cover and keep warm.

Deglaze the pan with vinegar, stock, raspberry concentrate and shallots. Reduce the liquid by half over high heat.

Stir in the cornstarch mix. Add black pepper and berries. Serve the sauce over the chicken and garnish with more fresh raspberries.

Yield: 4 servings

185 calories / 3.36 grams fat per serving

CHICKEN WITH RED SESAME SAUCE

Ancho chiles are dried poblano peppers and are often used in commercial chili powders. They are available in the produce section or Mexican foods section of most groceries or health food stores.

1/2 cup sesame seeds
1 chile ancho, toasted, seeded, soaked in hot water
1 teaspoon cinnamon
A pinch of ground cloves
5 peppercorns
1 tablespoon vegetable oil
1 clove garlic
1/2 cup tomato puree
1/2 cup diced tomatoes
1/2 bottle chili sauce (available wherever you find catsup)
2 cups chicken stock
1/2 teaspoon salt
1 tablespoon vinegar
1 teaspoon sugar
8 four ounce boneless, skinless chicken breasts
Vegetable cooking spray

Toast the sesame seeds until golden in a dry skillet over medium heat. Puree in a blender, then saute briefly in oil.

Blend anchos, spices and garlic with a little of the chicken stock in a blender. Add to the sesame mixture and cook, stirring, for five minutes.

Puree the diced tomatoes and add, along with the tomato puree and chili sauce. Add remaining chicken stock until sauce is the desired consistency.

Saute chicken breasts with vegetable spray in a non stick skillet, browning both sides lightly. Add sauce and simmer for about five minutes. Serve, topped with sauce and a sprinkle of sesame seeds for garnish.

Yield: 8 servings (246 calories / 5 grams fat per serving)

GINGERED CHICKEN WITH MANGO SAUCE

This tasty tropical dish may not sail you to all the way to St. Johns, but you will be headed in the right direction.

6 four ounce boneless, skinless chicken breasts
1/2 cup unsweetened pineapple juice
1 tablespoon peeled, chopped fresh ginger
1 teaspoon soy sauce

Marinate the chicken in the juice, ginger and soy sauce.

Mango Sauce:
1 tablespoon olive oil
2 cloves garlic, minced
2 teaspoons ginger, minced
1 tablespoon honey
1/4 teaspoon ground cloves
1/4 teaspoon nutmeg
1 teaspoon soy sauce
1/2 cup strong chicken stock with 1 teaspoon cornstarch
1 cup mangoes, diced
1 teaspoon lemon zest
Juice of 1/2 lemon

Saute the garlic and ginger in the oil. Add the honey, seasonings, and chicken stock mixture and cook until slightly thickened. Add the remaining ingredients.

Grill the chicken and top with the sauce. Garnish with fresh chopped cilantro.

Yield: 6 servings

230 calories / 5.5 grams fat per serving

344

LIME GRILLED CHICKEN
WITH BLACK BEAN SAUCE

Canned black beans make this dish quick and easy. Simply marinate the chicken breasts before you leave in the morning, then assemble the sauce while the chicken grills.

2 tablespoons fresh lime juice
1 tablespoon vegetable oil
1/4 teaspoon cayenne
4 cloves garlic, minced
4 four ounce boneless, skinless chicken breasts

Place all the ingredients in a plastic storage bag and marinate, turning occasionally, for eight hours.

Grill chicken until done.

Black Bean Sauce:
1 cup drained, cooked black beans
1/2 cup orange juice
2 tablespoons balsamic vinegar
14 teaspoon salt
1/8 teaspoon freshly ground black pepper
2 cloves garlic, minced
Fresh cilantro for garnish

Blend the beans and remaining ingredients in a food processor. Simmer briefly in a small saucepan.

Garnish:
1/2 cup diced red bell peppers
1 tablespoon chopped purple onion

Blanch the bell pepper and onion briefly in boiling water, drain and set aside.

Serve the sauce over the grilled chicken and top with the peppers, onion and fresh cilantro.

Yield: 4 servings

245 calories / 6.5 grams fat per serving

PANEED CHICKEN
WITH CREOLE MUSTARD SAUCE

The trick here is to cook the coated chicken with enough heat to crisp the exterior, but not so much as to burn it. Try spraying each piece lightly before putting it into the skillet, don't try to cook too many pieces at once, and don't be afraid to peek. Your patience will be rewarded with a crunchy, golden, low fat crust. 'Paneed,' by the way, means 'breaded.'

The chicken:
4 four ounce boneless, skinless, chicken breasts, cut in half
1 cup buttermilk
2 egg whites
1 cup toasted whole wheat bread crumbs
1/3 cup grated Parmesan cheese
Vegetable cooking spray

Pound the chicken pieces out between two pieces of plastic wrap, using a rolling pin, until 1/4 inch thick.

Beat buttermilk and egg whites together in one bowl; combine the bread crumbs and cheese in another bowl.

Dip the chicken pieces first into the egg wash, then into the bread crumb mixture, coating thoroughly.

Spray the bottom of a non stick skillet with non stick spray and saute the chicken a couple of minutes per side over medium heat until golden brown. Serve with Creole Mustard Sauce on the next page.

CREOLE MUSTARD SAUCE:

1/3 cup evaporated skim milk
1/3 cup nonfat sour cream
1/4 cup creole mustard
1 teaspoon Worcestershire
1/2 teaspoon dry mustard
1/8 teaspoon black pepper
1/8 teaspoon white pepper
1/8 teaspoon dried basil
Pinch of cayenne

Combine all ingredients in a saucepan, heat gently through to combine flavors, then cool.

Yield: 4 servings

275 calories / 6.2 grams fat per serving

PAPRIKA CHICKEN

We commonly think of paprika as a coloring agent, but it also has an excellent flavor all it's own. The best, imported Hungarian, reminds one of toasted saffron and is well worth the extra expense in a dish like this.

4 teaspoons olive oil (divided)
4 large shitake mushrooms, sliced
4 chicken breasts, cut into 1/2-inch strips
1 red bell pepper, thinly sliced
3/4 cup onion, thinly sliced
2 cloves garlic, minced
2 teaspoons paprika
Pinch marjoram
1 teaspoon flour
1/2 cup chicken stock
1/2 cup nonfat yogurt
Pinch of cayenne pepper
2 tablespoons chopped parsley

Cook the mushrooms in two teaspoons of oil. Set aside.

Saute the chicken over high heat in the same skillet. Set aside the chicken with the mushrooms. Add remaining oil and saute peppers and onion until slightly browned.

Add garlic, paprika and marjoram. Cook one minute. Sprinkle on flour and stir. Add stock, cook over low heat for ten minutes.

Allow to cool and add half of the mixture with yogurt to food processor. Puree. Return all ingredients to heat and gently warm through. Garnish with parsley.

Yield: 4 servings

249 calories / 6.8 grams fat per serving

SIX PEPPER CHICKEN

Count yourself a "chilephile" if you can enumerate the six peppers used in this brightly colored but only slightly spicy dish. (Hint: the answer may be cut and dried but it is not black and white.)

6 boneless, skinless 4-ounce chicken breasts, pounded out to 1/4" thickness
1 green bell pepper, roasted, peeled, cut into thin strips
1 red bell pepper, roasted, peeled, cut into thin strips
1 yellow bell pepper, roasted, peeled, cut into thin strips
2 tablespoons blackening seasoning (1 tablespoon plus 1 teaspoon paprika, 1/2 teaspoon garlic powder, 1/2 teaspoon onion powder, 1/4 teaspoon black pepper, 1/8 teaspoon white pepper, 1/8 teaspoon cayenne pepper, 1/4 teaspoon oregano and 1/4 teaspoon thyme)
Vegetable cooking spray

Put a few strips of the roasted peppers lengthwise on the underside of the chicken breasts. Roll up and secure with toothpicks. Season with blackening mix and "blacken" briefly in a skillet over high heat with no-stick spray. Finish cooking on a sprayed baking sheet in a 400 degree oven for ten minutes. Remove the toothpicks, slice chicken into 1/2" rolls and serve the slightly overlapping slices on a bed of the sauce.

Sauce:
1 small ancho chile, seeded, soaked in warm water
3 tomatoes, charred on the grill
1/2 onion
1 clove garlic
1 teaspoon olive oil
1 cup tomato juice
1 can evaporated skim milk
1 tablespoon cornstarch, mixed with some of the milk
Juice of 1/2 lime
1 tablespoon cilantro, chopped

Puree chile, tomatoes, onion, garlic. Saute five minutes in oil. Add tomato juice and milk. Add cornstarch mix, cook until slightly thickened. Add lime juice and cilantro.

Yield: 6 servings

245 calories / 5.2 grams fat per serving

SMOKED TURKEY REUBENS

Holden Caulfield's favorite. A spicy non fat dressing, low fat swiss, and lean nitrate free turkey combine for this "keeper" in the rye.

6 tablespoons nonfat mayonnaise
2 tablespoons catsup
3 tablespoons skim milk
3 tablespoons minced onion
2 tablespoons chopped dill pickle
1 clove garlic, minced
1/4 teaspoon oregano
1/8 teaspoon cayenne pepper
2 tablespoons Dijon mustard
1 teaspoon honey
2 tablespoons fresh dill, minced
2 cups sauerkraut, drained and rinsed

Combine all ingredients.

24 slices rye or pumpernickel bread
12 ounces low fat Swiss cheese, thinly sliced
16 ounces smoked turkey breast, thinly sliced
Butter flavored vegetable cooking spray

Divide turkey, sauerkraut mixture and cheese onto 12 slices of bread. Top with other slices and grill, using no-stick spray in a skillet (partially covered), turning once, until cheese melts.

Yield: 12 servings

249 calories/ 7 grams fat per serving

Seafood

BLACKENED SALMON

This grilled version of a cajun classic retains all of the spicy crusty goodness in the original without any of the fat. In fact, the only advantage of the traditional method over this one is that it will give you a pretty good chance of getting better acquainted with the brave men and women of your local Fire Department. (Those of you who have tried that method will know what I mean.) So, try our version. It works well with almost any skinless fish filet, or chicken breast.

Our apologies to Paul Prudhomme...

4 four ounce salmon filets, skin removed
4 tablespoons paprika
2 teaspoons onion powder
2 teaspoons garlic powder
1 teaspoon cayenne powder
1 teaspoon white pepper
1 teaspoon black pepper
1 teaspoon thyme
1 teaspoon oregano
2 teaspoons salt (optional)
Vegetable cooking spray

Combine seasonings in a medium bowl. Pat fish dry, then dredge in the seasonings, coating thoroughly.

Spray both sides of the filet with the vegetable spray and grill, turning occasionally until "blackened" and done. (Approximately 10 minutes per inch over a fairly hot grill.)

Serve with a lemon wedge or brush with a little melted margarine.

Yield: 4 servings

161 calories / 6.1 grams fat per serving

BLUE CORNMEAL BATTERED TROUT

If you have ever been so fortunate as to find yourself camped out in the mountains of Colorado or New Mexico dipping a freshly caught, cornmeal battered trout to sizzle in a skillet over an open fire, then you know, as they say, "It just doesn't get any better than this." The American rainbow trout is one of the world's great eating fish, and the commercially raised ones, now widely available, are excellent.

6 four ounce rainbow trout filets
4 egg whites
1/8 tcaspoon cumin
1/8 teaspoon dried basil
1/8 teaspoon garlic powder
1/4 teaspoon baking soda
12 ounces flat beer
3 cups blue cornmeal
Vegetable cooking spray

Lightly beat the egg whites in a large mixing bowl. Whisk in successively, the baking soda, seasonings, beer and cornmeal.

Dip filets in batter and using the vegetable spray, saute in a skillet over medium high heat, skin side up. Turn once to finish.

Serve with a lemon wedge or the Red Chile Tartar Sauce on page 79.

Yield: 6 servings

163 calories / 3.8 grams fat per serving

CRABMEAT ENCHILADAS

Mexico, with its extensive coastlines along two oceans has a rich (and too often overlooked) tradition of seafood cookery. 'Salsaed' oysters on the half shell, shredded shark tacos, and enchiladas filled with crabmeat are all typical of fare you might expect to find there.

1 teaspoon margarine
1/4 cup chopped green onions
1/4 cup chopped red pepper
1/4 cup chopped green pepper
3 medium tomatoes, peeled, seeded and chopped
1/4 cup canned green chiles
1 pound fresh lump crab meat, drained and cleaned*
1 tablespoon minced fresh cilantro
1 teaspoon minced fresh oregano
1 tablespoon fresh lime juice
1 tablespoon chopped green olives
Vegetable cooking spray
12 blue corn tortillas

Coat a large non stick skillet with the spray. Add margarine and melt over low heat. Saute the onion and peppers until tender. Add the tomatoes and green chilies and simmer for 5 minutes, stirring occasionally.

Add the crab and cook until thoroughly heated, 3-4 minutes, without stirring. Remove from heat and gently stir in the fresh herbs, olives and lime juice.

Drain each portion with a slotted spoon and place equal portions in the corn tortillas. (Warm the corn tortillas first by wrapping in plastic and then in a moist towel. Microwave for one minute.)

Tightly roll each tortilla and place seam side down in an oven proof casserole dish. Top with Roasted Red Pepper sauce, page 80 and bake at 350 degrees for ten minutes. Top with one tablespoon of Mock Sour Cream, page 63, before serving. Garnish with fresh cilantro and an olive slice.

Yield: 6 servings (two enchiladas each)

240 calories / 2.3 grams fat per serving

*Be sure to examine the crab meat carefully and remove any pieces of shell.

Contributed by Trisha Shirey

CRABMEAT QUESADILLAS WITH MANGO SALSA

Fresh or frozen crab is a must for this recipe. The canned stuff is as stringy and tasteless as Sandra Bernhardt.

The sunny golden color and spicy, sweet, snap of the mango salsa make a nice addition, but the verde and red pepper salsas in this book would work well also. Better yet, make them all and let everyone customize their quesadillas.

2 ounces low fat cheddar, grated
3 ounces low fat cottage cheese
2 tablespoons Parmesan cheese
1 teaspoon cumin
1 large clove garlic, minced
1/2 serrano pepper, seeded and minced
6 ounces lump crab meat
3 thinly sliced red bell pepper rings
4 whole wheat flour tortillas
Vegetable cooking spray

Combine the first six ingredients. Fold in the crab and spread the mixture on one tortilla, top with the bell pepper rings and then with the other tortilla.

Spray a non stick pan with the vegetable spray. Cook the quesadilla over medium heat, covered, for three or four minutes, until bottom is slightly browned.

Invert with a spatula and cook until underside browns.

Cut into fourths and serve with the Mango Salsa on page 75.

Yield: 8 servings

280 calories / 6.3 grams fat per serving

CRAWFISH IN PHYLLO PASTRY

Everyone should try their hand at phyllo pastry at least once. It's easier than it looks and the finished product is very impressive. Look for phyllo in the frozen foods section in most grocery stores. Substitute fresh cooked shrimp if you can't find crawfish meat.

1 pound shelled crawfish meat, cooked
1 tablespoon corn oil margarine
1/2 cup minced onion
1 clove garlic, minced
1/2 cup chopped mushrooms
1/4 cup finely diced green peppers
1/4 cup finely diced celery
1 package phyllo pastry, thawed according to directions
Vegetable cooking spray

Saute vegetables in margarine over medium heat until softened.

Add the crawfish and cook for two minutes.

Follow the instructions on the pastry box for handling the phyllo, substituting the vegetable spray for the melted butter called for.

Using one sheet per serving, fold the pastry first in half lengthwise. Spray with non stick. Place the filling at one end and fold the phyllo over to form a triangle. Continue folding the pastry in triangles until the entire strip is folded and the edges are sealed. Spray with non stick spray and place on a baking sheet.

Bake at 375 degrees until golden brown. Serve with Cajun Demiglace sauce on page 61. Pool the sauce on a plate, place crawfish phyllos on top and sprinkle with minced chives.

Yield: 4 servings

245 calories / 4.8 grams fat per serving, with sauce

DORADO VERACRUZANO

This savory Mexican classic balances an intriguing combination of contrasting flavors, colors, and textures.

"Dorado" means golden and refers to the luminescent skin on the fish we call dolphin fish or mahi mahi. (No relation to Flipper!) However, almost any fish or crustacean pairs wonderfully with this sauce.

2 tablespoons olive oil
1 onion, diced
2 cloves garlic, minced
1 large red bell pepper, large dice
1 large green bell pepper, large dice
6 green olives, chopped
2 tablespoons capers, rinsed and drained
1 cup golden raisins
1 cup tomato puree
6 tomatoes, skins charred in the broiler or over an open flame
1 bay leaf, crushed
1 cup white wine
1/4 teaspoon cinnamon
1 tablespoon minced jalapeño
6 four ounce fish skinless filets (mahi mahi, snapper)

Brown the onion in oil over medium high heat. Add the garlic and bell peppers and saute briefly.

Crush the tomatoes in a food processor and add to the sauteed vegetables, then add remaining ingredients, except fish.

Simmer to a sauce-like consistency and poach fish in this sauce. Poach ten minutes per inch of thickness of the filet, measured at the widest point. Serve the sauce spooned over the fish.

Yield: 6 servings

139 calories / 1.8 grams fat per serving (when using mahi mahi)

POTATO WRAPPED SALMON WITH LIME, GINGER, AND LEEK SAUCE

An unusual, delicious dish with a nifty presentation. The real trick here is in getting the potato slices thin enough to be truly pliable. A commercial style slicer is ideal; the wide blade side on a four sided grater will suffice.

6 four ounce boneless, skinless salmon filets
2 tablespoons finely minced onion
2 teaspoons fresh thyme, minced
Pinch allspice
Pinch cayenne pepper
3 potatoes, peeled, sliced paper thin, soaked in a water-lemon mixture (4
　　to 1)
Vegetable cooking spray

Season fish with the first four ingredients.

Blot potato slices dry. Arrange into six rectangular mats, overlapping the slices. Place a piece of fish in the center of each one, bring up the sides to overlap; invert.

Using the spray, saute folded side down over medium high heat for a couple of minutes. Invert and saute one minute. Place on a sprayed baking sheet to finish, and bake at 425 degrees for 10 minutes.

Sauce:
1 tablespoon fresh ginger, minced
1 tablespoon garlic, minced
1/2 leek, cleaned and thinly sliced
1 teaspoon vegetable oil
1 tablespoon cornstarch
1 pint chicken stock
3 tablespoons lime juice
2 tablespoons brown sugar

Saute the ginger, garlic and leek in oil. Dissolve the cornstarch in a little of the stock. Simmer all together adding cornstarch as needed.

Yield: 6 servings

265 calories / 7 grams fat per serving

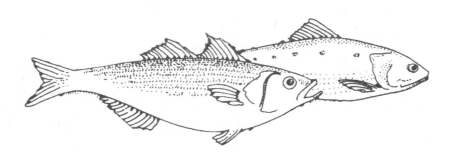

SALMON POTATO CROQUETTES

A great way to use leftover salmon. Serve with a bright green vegetable. A bowl of Borscht makes a good beginning and serves to remind us of those dishes which trace their roots to the Soviet Union or whatever they call the Soviet Union now that they don't call the Soviet Union the Soviet Union anymore...

9 ounces cooked, flaked salmon
6 ounces potato, peeled, shredded and parboiled for 1 minute
1 egg, beaten
2 egg whites, beaten
2 tablespoons grated onion
1 tablespoon lemon juice
1 teaspoon Worcestershire sauce
1 ounce Parmesan cheese
1/2 teaspoon grated lemon zest
Pinch of cayenne pepper
1 tablespoon minced fresh dill (or 1 1/2 teaspoon dried dill)

Combine all ingredients, shape into patties.

Using a non stick skillet or griddle and non stick spray, brown patties on both sides.

Serve with Mock Sour Cream (page 72) and a lemon wedge.

Yield: 4 servings

202 calories per / 6 grams fat per serving

SEAFOOD DIRTY RICE

Neptune's version of another Louisiana legacy. This reheats well in the microwave, if there's any left and there won't be.

If you want to retreat from "dirty" to "suggestive", just reduce the cayenne.

1 tablespoon margarine
1 teaspoon vegetable oil
1/2 cup tomato sauce
3 tablespoons finely diced onion
2 1/2 tablespoons finely diced bell pepper
2 tablespoons finely diced celery
1 teaspoon finely minced garlic
1/8 teaspoon salt
1 teaspoon white pepper
1 teaspoon thyme
1/2 teaspoon cayenne
1 1/2 cups seafood stock*
1/3 cup half and half
1/2 teaspoon cornstarch
3 cups cooked rice
3/4 cup minced green onion
1 1/4 pounds small shrimp, peeled
3/4 cup crab meat, picked over and shells removed

Melt margarine and oil in a large skillet. Saute vegetables, tomato sauce and seasonings for five minutes, stirring frequently. Add stock, and cook ten minutes.

Mix the cornstarch and the half and half and add to the sauce, simmer for five minutes.

Add the shrimp and simmer for three minutes.

Add the rice and green onions. When fully heated, gently fold in the crab meat and serve.

*To make a quick seafood stock, simmer the shrimp shells in 1 1/2 cups of clam juice for 10 minutes and strain.

Yield: 6 servings

275 calories per / 4.5 grams fat per serving

SHRIMP CREOLE

A word or two about roux; exercise caution. They don't call it "cajun napalm" for nothing. The finished roux should be very dark, with an almost purple sheen to it; making it without scorching requires your complete, undivided attention. So, kick the kids and the dog outside, and if the phone rings, let it. You have work to do.

3 tablespoons vegetable oil
1/4 cup flour
5 garlic cloves, minced
1 cup finely diced onion
1/2 cup finely diced bell pepper
1/2 cup finely diced celery
1 quart seafood stock (or clam juice simmered with shrimp shells, then
      strained)
1/2 cup chopped parsley
1 cup tomato puree
2 cups canned diced tomatoes
1 1/2 bay leaves
1 teaspoon thyme
1/2 teaspoon tabasco
1 1/4 pound okra, sliced
Non stick spray
2 teaspoons Worcestershire sauce
2 pounds medium shrimp, peeled

Combine flour and oil in a heavy skillet and cook over medium low heat, stirring continuously, until the roux is a dark chocolate color.

Stir in the vegetables and cook until well coated and slightly softened.

Heat the stock in a large pot. Whisk in the roux mixture. Add the tomato products and seasonings. Simmer for thirty minutes.

Saute the okra briefly in a skillet, using non stick spray. Add to the pot and simmer for one hour. Add the worcestershire and shrimp and cook until shrimp are just done, about ten minutes. Serve with 1/2 cup cooked rice.

Yield: 8 servings (1 1/2 cups creole and 1/2 cup rice)

275 calories / 7 grams fat per serving

SAN ANTONIO BAY CRABCAKES

Simple and delicious, these will disappear off of your plate faster than if the crab meat was still inside the crab.

2 egg whites
2 tablespoons nonfat mayonnaise
2 teaspoons Dijon mustard
Pinch cayenne
1/4 teaspoon worcestershire sauce
1 pound flaked crab meat, cleaned thoroughly
1/4 cup parsley
1/4 cup minced green onion
8 soda crackers, crushed
1 serrano pepper, seeded and minced
Butter flavored non stick spray

Combine the first five ingredients, then fold in the remaining ingredients. Shape into twelve patties, put on foil, cover and chill.

Saute in a non stick pan with butter flavored non stick spray until crisp. Serve with lime wedges, and chipotle mayonnaise, page 65.

Yield: 6 servings

105 calories/ 3 grams fat per serving

SPICY FISH

If you are sensitive about such things, you may reduce the amount of chiles in this Orientally oriented dish to prevent an Occidental overdose.

4 four ounce orange roughy filets

Marinade:
2 green onions, chopped
2 tablespoons low sodium soy sauce (or use 1 tablespoon regular soy
    sauce)
1 clove garlic, minced
1 teaspoon sesame seed oil
3-4 slices fresh ginger root
1/4 teaspoon crushed dried red chilies
1/4 teaspoon cracked black pepper
1/4 cup clam juice
Vegetable coating spray

Combine all marinade ingredients and pour over fish. Refrigerate for 30 minutes to 2 hours.

Place fish on a baking sheet that has been sprayed with non stick spray. Bake at 375 degrees for ten minutes per inch of thickness of filets. (Measure at the thickest area of the filet. Fold the thinner end of the filet under before cooking, so that it doesn't get overdone.)

This is also good for tuna, shark, or swordfish cooked on a grill. Use the marinade for basting the fish while grilling.

Yield: 4 servings

179 calories/ 8 grams fat per serving

Contributed by Trisha Shirey

TIMBALE OF BAY SCALLOPS
WITH SPINACH AND RED PEPPER SAUCE

This is an upscale presentation piece that you might want to serve for company. The color combinations are quite striking and the pepper and orange zest lend an interesting flavor to the dish.

1 pound bay scallops
1 teaspoon serrano pepper, seeded and minced
1 teaspoon minced orange zest
1/2 cup shallots, minced
1 clove garlic, minced
1 red or yellow bell pepper, roasted*
12 ounces spinach, blanched, drained and squeezed dry*

Put scallops in a bowl with serrano, orange zest, shallots and garlic and marinate overnight. Roast, then peel the red pepper and cut out four one-inch rounds and place, peeled side down into soup ramekins.

Surround with five scallops, top with half of the spinach, pressing slightly. Layer remaining scallops and then spinach.

Cover and steam for ten minutes. To serve, uncover, and run a knife around the edge, and pour off any accumulated liquid and invert onto a plate lined with the sauce below.

RED PEPPER SAUCE:
2 red bell peppers, chopped
1/4 large onion, chopped
1 clove garlic, minced
Pinch of cayenne
1 1/2 teaspoons vegetable oil
1 1/2 teaspoons red wine vinegar
1 1/2 teaspoons lemon juice

Combine all ingredients and simmer, covered, until soft, about thirty minutes. Cool, puree and strain.

*see glossary for Blanching instructions and Roasting Peppers

Yield: 4 servings

155 calories / 2 grams fat per serving

TORTILLA CRUSTED GULF SNAPPER

Any firm fleshed white fish filet will substitute nicely, but if you use snapper, specify "red" or "gulf" snapper; not the less desirable western rockfish some malodorous marketing magnate misnamed "Pacific Coast Snapper".

4 four ounce skinless red snapper filets, no more than 1/3" thick*
1/2 cup flour
2 egg whites, beaten with 3/4 cup buttermilk
6 corn tortillas, cut into very, very thin strips
2 teaspoons olive oil
Vegetable cooking spray

Dredge fish in flour, then egg wash, then really press in and coat with tortilla strips.

Spray the coated fish with vegetable spray and saute gently in olive oil over medium heat, in a non stick skillet, turning as needed so that the tortillas crisp without burning.

Serve with Chipotle Mayonnaise, page 65.

Yield: 4 servings

194 calories / 3.4 grams fat per serving

*You may butterfly (see Glossary) filets if necessary to achieve the desired thickness.

BOUILLABAISSE WITH SPINACH RAVIOLI

Whether you call it a soup, a stew or a seafood pasta dish, this healthy and hearty concoction should satisfy the most ravenous or discriminating appetite.

The Soup:
1 tablespoon olive oil
1/2 onion, minced
2 leeks, cleaned and sliced
1 carrot, diced
1 stalk of celery, diced
3 cloves garlic, minced
1 bay leaf
1 teaspoon thyme
1/2 teaspoon basil
1/2 teaspoon fennel seed
2/3 cup white wine
16 ounces canned tomatoes, pureed
1 tablespoon tomato paste
3-inch strip of orange peel
1 quart seafood stock (or clam juice)
Juice of 1 lemon
2 tablespoons Pernod
Pinch of cayenne pepper
1 1/2 pounds assorted seafood, cut into pieces (fish, shrimp, crab, lobster, mussels, etc.)

Saute vegetables briefly in oil.

Add remaining ingredients, except seafood, and simmer for 30 minutes. Just before serving, add seafood and cover, cooking until just done.

The Ravioli:
1 package of won ton wrappers
12 ounce package fresh spinach, stemmed, cleaned, blanched and pressed free of all liquid, then chopped
1 clove garlic, minced
2 tablespoons Parmesan cheese

Combine spinach, garlic and cheese. Follow directions on won ton package using this mixture as a filling. Simmer in a little of the seafood stock. Set aside and cover. When you are ready to serve, place two won tons in the bottom of a wide soup bowl and spoon bouillabaisse over top.

Yield: 6 servings (294 calories / 5.8 grams fat per serving)

CIOPPINO

This is a dish worthy of dinner guests and the little bit of extra trouble it takes to prepare.

Be sure to use a full flavored stock. You can make the soup part of this dish ahead of time, adding everything but the seafood; it freezes well.

It would be traditional to come up with your own combination of seafood ingredients. Try to include at lest two types of fish, one crustacean, (shrimp, lobster, etc.) and one bivalve (mussels or clams).

Oh, by the way, the "Ci" in Cioppino is pronounced "chee" as in Cheetoes or cheeseburger. Or cheap shot.

2 tablespoons olive oil
2 cups finely diced onion
1 large leek, cleaned and finely chopped (white part, plus a little of the
      green)
1/2 cup finely diced celery
2 tablespoons garlic
16 ounces tomato paste
2 cups canned chopped tomatoes, with juice
2 teaspoons crushed saffron
1 tablespoon fresh thyme (or 1 1/2 teaspoon dried)
1 tablespoon Pernod (optional)
1 teaspoon crushed fennel seeds
4 to 5 cups fish stock*
1 pound peeled shrimp
1 pound fish filets, cut into bite sized pieces
16 scrubbed mussels
Tabasco to taste
Black pepper to taste

In a large pot, saute the onion, leek, celery and garlic in olive oil over medium heat until softened. Add all other ingredients except seafood and simmer for 30 minutes.

Add the seafood and simmer, covered, until the mussels open and fish and shrimp are just done. Divide into large soup bowls and serve with crusty French bread.

Yield: 12 servings

232 calories / 2.4 grams fat per serving

* Bottled clam juice may be used, or simmer some carrots, celery and onion with the shrimp shells for fifteen minutes. Drain and use.

JAMBALAYA

There are probably as many Jambalaya recipes as there are Louisiana bayous down which they may be procured; all of them good, but most, alas, too high in fat to be eaten regularly with a clear conscience. Our version uses an ultra lean sausage; use a little lean diced nitrate free ham if a similar product is not available to you. And if you ever order this dish in Louisiana backwater country, think twice about anybody who offers a "free 'deliverance' service".

2 bay leaves
1 teaspoon salt
1 teaspoon cayenne
2 teaspoons oregano
1 teaspoon white pepper
1/2 teaspoon black pepper
1 teaspoon thyme
2 tablespoons vegetable oil
1 cup Carabeef* sausage, sliced
1 1/2 cups chopped onion
1 cup chopped celery
3/4 cup chopped bell pepper
3/4 cup chicken breast, cut into bite sized pieces
2 cups diced tomatoes and juice
1/2 cup tomato puree
5 cups chicken or seafood stock
1/2 cup minced green onion
2 cups uncooked brown rice
1 dozen shrimp, peeled and coarsely chopped
1 dozen oysters, in their liquid, coarsely chopped

Saute sausage and chicken briefly in oil. Add onion, celery, bell pepper and saute. Add seasonings and garlic.

Add tomato products, cook 5 minutes, stirring. Add stock, bring to a boil; stir in green onions, rice, seafood.

Bake in a covered pan at 350 degrees for one hour.

Yield: 1 gallon

226 calories / 2.2 grams fat per 4 ounce serving

Desserts

BLUEBERRY SPICE CAKE WITH MOCHA GLAZE

This is a comfortable, down home dessert that just about everyone seems to love. It freezes well.

1 1/4 cups flour
1/2 teaspoon baking powder
1/2 teaspoon baking soda
1/2 teaspoon cinnamon
1/8 teaspoon nutmeg
1 cup rolled oats
2 1/2 ounces soft tofu, well drained
3/4 cup brown sugar
2 eggs and 1 egg white
1 cup unsweetened applesauce
1 cup blueberries, thawed if frozen
Vegetable cooking spray

Preheat the oven to 350 degrees. Spray an 8 x 8 baking pan with vegetable spray.

Combine flour, baking powder, soda, spices, and oats. Set aside.

Blend tofu until smooth. Blend in sugar, then eggs one at a time, then applesauce. Stir tofu mix and blueberries into dry ingredients. Mix only until dry ingredients are moistened.

Pour batter into pan. Bake at 350 degrees for 30 to 35 minutes or until cake tester comes out clean.

Cool cake in pan. Use a toothpick or a cake tester to put small holes all over the top of the cake to allow the glaze to soak into the cake.

Glaze:
1/4 cup powdered sugar
2 teaspoons instant coffee
2 tablespoons water
1 teaspoon cornstarch
1 teaspoon vanilla

Combine the first four ingredients in a small saucepan and blend until smooth. Heat until slightly thickened, stirring constantly. Add vanilla and spread over cooled cake.

Yield: 12 servings

109 calories/ 2 grams fat per serving

Contributed by Trisha Shirey

CARROT CAKE WITH BAVARIAN CREAM

Serve still warm with the chilled cream for dessert or as a holiday breakfast.

2 cups whole wheat pastry flour
1 1/2 teaspoons baking powder
2/3 teaspoon cinnamon
1/4 teaspoon baking soda
1/8 teaspoon nutmeg
2 eggs
2 teaspoons vegetable oil
1 1/2 cups carrots, grated
3/4 cup egg whites
1/2 cup honey
1/4 cup apple juice

Combine dry ingredients.

Combine eggs and oil, add dry ingredients, whip three minutes. Add carrots.

Whip honey and egg whites until medium firm; fold into carrot mixture. Pour into a Bundt cake pan and bake at 350 degrees for 20-25 minutes.

BAVARIAN CREAM:
1/4 cup maple syrup
1/3 cup ricotta cheese
1/3 cup nonfat yogurt
1/4 teaspoon vanilla
1/2 teaspoon gelatin, dissolved in 1 teaspoon warm water

Blend all ingredients until smooth. Mix a little yogurt-cheese mix into gelatin, then fold all together. Chill. Serve with a dollop on each piece of cake.

Yield: 12 servings

133 calories / 1.2 grams fat per serving

CHOCOLATE ANGEL FOOD CAKE

Nothing with no fat was ever this good. Try it with a little kahlua drizzled over the top.

1/4 cup unsweetened cocoa powder
1/4 cup hot strong coffee (chocolate almond is best)
1 1/4 cups sugar
3/4 cup sifted cake flour
12 egg whites
1 teaspoon cream of tartar

Preheat oven to 350 degrees. Dissolve the cocoa in the hot coffee and allow to cool.

Sift together the sugar, flour and salt. Set aside.

Beat the egg whites until frothy. Add the cream of tartar and whip on high speed until stiff. Fold the flour mixture into the whites one third at a time.

Combine one third of the egg white mixture with the coffee and cocoa mixture. Fold this mixture back into the rest of the egg whites, mixing gently.

Pour the batter into an ungreased tube pan. Remove air bubbles in the batter by pulling a knife around the pan.

Bake at 350 degrees for 50 to 60 minutes. Cake will crack on the top and cracks should feel dry and spring back lightly when touched.

Cool the cake upside-down in the pan on a funnel or bottle so that the cake does not touch the counter. Run a knife around the pan to loosen the cake.

Yield: 16 servings
86 calories / 0 grams fat per serving

Contributed by Trisha Shirey

CHOCOLATE TORTE

If we had to pick the one most requested new recipe, this would be it. The prune puree serves to replace the fat, but unless you say something, no one will believe anything is missing from this rich, dark, densely chocolate cake. It freezes well.

2 cups flour
1 cup unsweetened cocoa powder
2 cups sugar
2 teaspoons baking soda
1 teaspoon baking powder
1/4 teaspoon salt
1/2 teaspoon cinnamon
4 (2.5 ounces each) jars baby food pureed prunes
2 teaspoons vanilla
2 eggs, beaten
1 cup skim milk
1 cup strong coffee
Vegetable cooking spray
Powdered sugar

Preheat oven to 350 degrees.

Sift together the flour, cocoa, sugar, baking soda, baking powder, and salt in a large mixing bowl.

Add the prunes, vanilla, eggs, milk and stir just until blended.

Stir coffee into the batter until blended. Pour the batter into 2 nine inch baking pans or springform pans that have been sprayed with vegetable spray.

Bake for 30 to 35 minutes, or until center tests done with a toothpick. Let the cakes cool in pans for 10 minutes. Invert onto a wire rack to cool.

Sift powdered sugar over the top of the cake before slicing.

Yield: 12 servings per cake (141 calories / 1.25 gram fat per serving)

DOUBLE GINGER SPICE CAKE
WITH ORANGE GINGER SAUCE

Once again, as in the previous recipe, the prune puree replaces much of the fat you might expect to find in a recipe like this. Where do you get prune puree? We use baby food prunes. (Let's just let that be our little secret.)

1/2 teaspoon ground black pepper
1 1/2 cups flour
1 teaspoon baking soda
1 teaspoon ground ginger
1 teaspoon ground cinnamon
1/2 teaspoon salt
2 tablespoons margarine
4 ounces prune puree
1/2 cup packed brown sugar
1 egg
2 egg whites
1/4 cup dark molasses
2/3 cup buttermilk
1/4 cup crystallized ginger, chopped
Vegetable cooking spray

Preheat oven to 325 degrees. Spray and flour an 8-inch pan.
Combine first six ingredients.

Cream margarine until light. Beat in sugar. Beat in egg. Beat in egg whites. Mix in prune puree and molasses. Add half of the dry ingredients, then the buttermilk and other half. Fold in crystallized ginger. Bake about 45 minutes.

Serve with orange ginger sauce and a dollop of frozen vanilla yogurt.

ORANGE GINGER SAUCE:

3 large oranges, peeled and segmented
1 cup orange juice and 2 tablespoons (some from segmenting)
6 tablespoons sugar
1 cinnamon stick
3 tablespoons crystallized ginger, chopped

Cook juice, sugar, cinnamon to syrup. Strain over oranges and ginger.

Yield: 12 servings

128 calories / 2.5 grams fat per serving

GINGERBREAD

Old fashioned goodness from new fangled ingredients.   The tofu lowers the fat content and raises the nutritional value without sacrificing moistness or flavor.

2 ounces tofu, drained
1 ounce (2 tablespoons) margarine, softened
2 1/4 teaspoons vegetable oil
Vegetable cooking spray
Flour

Preheat oven to 325 degrees. Spray a 6 by 10 baking dish with vegetable spray and coat lightly with flour. In a blender or food processor, blend tofu until smooth. Transfer to a mixing bowl and add margarine and oil. Cream well with a mixer.

1 tablespoon brown sugar, packed
1 large egg or 2 egg whites
2/3 cup boiling water
2/3 cup dark molasses
1 1/4 cups flour
3/4 teaspoon baking soda
3/4 teaspoon ground ginger
1 teaspoon ground cinnamon
Pinch nutmeg
Powdered sugar

Beat the sugar and egg together until creamy. Stir in the boiling water and molasses, then add the tofu mixture.

Sift together the dry ingredients, then fold into the egg and sugar mixture until just blended.

Pour into prepared pan and bake for 30 to 40 minutes until a toothpick inserted in the center comes out clean.

Cool the cake and dust with powdered sugar.

Yield: 10 servings (2 x 3 inch square)

94 calories / 4 grams fat per serving

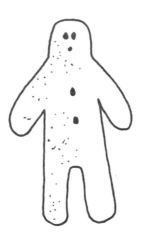

LEMON ROLL WITH BLACKBERRY SAUCE

Elegant pinwheel swirls of fat free Genoise cake in lemon custard floating on a shimmering pool of blackberry sauce are a picture and palate perfect finish.

Filling:
3 tablespoons cornstarch
1/3 cup sugar
1 teaspoon lemon zest
1/2 cup lemon juice
3/4 cup water
1 egg yolk
1 tablespoon margarine

In a small saucepan, combine cornstarch and sugar. Whisk in the lemon zest, juice and water. Cook until thickened. Mix a little of the sauce with the beaten egg yolk, then pour back into sauce. Stir over low heat for 2 minutes. Cool.

Cake:
Vegetable spray and flour for pan
5 egg whites
1/8 teaspoon salt
1/8 teaspoon cream of tartar
1/2 cup sugar
1/2 cup sifted cake flour
2 teaspoons lemon juice
1/2 teaspoon vanilla
1/4 teaspoon almond extract
3 tablespoons powdered sugar

Line a 10 by 15 baking sheet with foil. Thoroughly spray with vegetable spray and flour.

Beat egg whites, salt, and cream of tartar to very soft peaks. With a spatula, fold in granulated sugar, a spoonful at a time. Sift 1/2 of flour over and fold in. Repeat. Fold in the lemon juice and vanilla extract. Spread in the prepared pan and bake for 25 minutes at 300 degrees.

Sift half of the powdered sugar over the baked cake. Cover with a tea towel and invert onto another baking sheet. Carefully remove the top pan and foil. Trim the edges. Roll up in a towel, jellyroll style, while still warm.

(The recipe can be prepared one day ahead to this point.) Unroll the cake, remove the towel and spread with the filling, re-roll, and sift with the remaining powdered sugar. Slice into one inch thick roulades and serve in a pool of blackberry sauce. (See Raspberry Sauce, page 266)

Yield: 16 servings

99 calories / 1 gram fat per serving

LEMON CUSTARD CAKE

Title not withstanding, this luscious confectionery is anything but a "lemon".

1 cup sugar
6 tablespoons flour
Pinch of salt
1 tablespoon melted margarine
3/4 tablespoon grated lemon zest
6 tablespoons lemon juice
2 egg yolks
Egg substitute equivalent to two eggs
4 ounces tofu
2-1/2 cups 1/2% milk
6 egg whites

Combine flour, sugar and salt. Beat tofu, yolks and egg substitute until smooth. Incorporate zest, margarine, and juice into tofu mixture. Add milk. Combine in flour mixture. Beat egg whites until stiff; fold into lemon mixture. Pour into custard cups and bake in a waterbath at 350 degrees for 45 minutes/1 hour until top is golden and springs back to the touch. Chill. Serve with raspberry sauce (page 266).

Yield: 10 servings

96 calories/ 2.8 grams fat per serving

RASPBERRY CHARLOTTE

This dessert is definitely sophisticated enough for your next dinner party, but probably too good to wait that long. You might freeze the angel food cake slightly to make it easier to cut before proceeding with the rest of the recipe.

1 Angel food cake, crusts trimmed and cut into 1/3 inch slices
6 cups raspberries, fresh or frozen (thawed)
2/3 cup sugar
Vegetable cooking spray

Lightly coat sides and bottom of a spring form baking pan with spray. Spread slightly overlapping slices of cake to cover the bottom and sides of the pan, pressing gently for adherence.

Simmer sugar with berries until it dissolves. Spoon mixture onto cake, and top with remaining cake slices.

Cover with waxed paper, weight top down with a plate and a heavy object for 36 hours. Unmold, slice and serve with a dollop of frozen nonfat vanilla or raspberry yogurt.

Yield: 16 servings

141 calories / 0 grams fat per serving

AMARETTO CHIFFON CHEESECAKE

To be certain that this easy and elegant dessert cuts neatly, use a firm yogurt cheese and chill the cheesecake for at least six hours before slicing.

1 cup "Grapenuts" cereal, crushed in a blender or food processor
1 tablespoon margarine, softened
4 cups firm yogurt cheese (see the glossary)
2 envelopes gelatin
8 ounces unsweetened crushed pineapple, drained
6 ounces apple juice concentrate
1/2 cup water
1 tablespoon vanilla
1 tablespoon Amaretto liqueur
3 pasteurized egg whites, beaten stiff
1 12 ounce jar of "fruit only" apricot preserves

Mix the cereal and margarine and mold into a springform pan.

Mix the pineapple and gelatin. Bring the apple juice concentrate and water to a boil in a small saucepan and pour over the pineapple mixture. Stir to dissolve the gelatin.

Cool, add yogurt cheese, vanilla and Amaretto. Mix gently and then fold in the beaten egg whites.

Spread over the crumb crust and smooth the top with a spatula. Chill for at least six hours.

Warm the apricot preserves, just enough to soften, and use to glaze the cheesecake.

Yield: 16 servings

118 calories / 1 gram fat per serving

LEMONY CHEESECAKE

The cornstarch and eggs stabilize the yogurt cheese during the baking process, resulting in a dense, lemony, "deli-style" cheesecake. Garnish with a fresh strawberry.

Zest of two lemons
1/2 cup sugar
2 cups nonfat yogurt cheese (see the glossary listing)
Juice of two lemons
1 tablespoon cornstarch
2 eggs, lightly beaten
1 teaspoon lemon extract
Vegetable cooking spray

Preheat oven to 350 degrees. Lightly spray an eight or nine inch pie pan with vegetable spray.

Combine lemon zest and sugar in a food processor or blender and process until zest is ground completely.

Combine yogurt cheese, beaten eggs, cornstarch, extract and sugar, and lemon juice and mix well with a wire whisk or fork.

Pour into the prepared pan and smooth the top surface. Bake until the center is firm, about 25 to 30 minutes. Allow to cool before slicing.

Yield: 8 servings

126 calories / 1 gram fat per serving

Contributed by Trisha Shirey

LEMON CHIFFON

No dessert section would be complete without at least one recipe that incorporates Jello as an ingredient. We generally serve ours frozen, but it works just as well simply refrigerated.

1 1/2 cups evaporated skim milk, chilled
1 three ounce package lemon Jello gelatin
1 1/2 cups boiling water
1/2 cup sugar
1/4 cup lemon juice (2 lemons)
1 1/2 cups vanilla wafers (about 20), crushed finely*

Place the milk in a medium glass or stainless steel mixing bowl and chill in the freezer for 20 minutes.

Dissolve the gelatin in the boiling water and chill until partially set.

Place all but 1/4 cup of the vanilla wafer crumbs in a 9 x 13 baking dish.

Whip the chilled milk until it is tripled in volume and it resembles whipped cream.

When the gelatin is partially set, stir in the sugar and lemon juice. Fold the gelatin mixture gently into the whipped milk. Pour into the prepared baking dish and top with the remaining crumbs.

Chill until set, about two hours. It will set up more quickly in the freezer.

Yield: 20 servings

85 calories / 1 gram fat per serving

*Substitute gingersnaps, if desired, for a delicious variation. You may also omit the cookies for a nonfat dessert. Omit the sugar and replace with a sugar substitute to lower the calories.

Contributed by Trisha Shirey

ANGEL KISSES

These cookies will melt in your mouth. Serve them crushed over ice cream or frozen yogurt. Thanks to Shirley Mixen for her perseverance with this recipe.

1 1/2 cups ground almonds
9 large egg whites
1 1/2 teaspoons cream of tartar
1/8 teaspoon salt
2/3 cup sugar
1 tablespoon almond extract
1/2 teaspoon vanilla
Vegetable cooking spray

Preheat oven to 300 degrees. Bake the almonds on an ungreased baking sheet until lightly browned, about 10 minutes. Stir almonds occasionally while cooking. Remove from heat and allow to cool.

Place the egg whites in a glass or metal mixing bowl that is grease free. Add the salt and beat the egg whites until foamy. Add the cream of tartar, then gradually add the sugar until the egg whites will hold stiff peaks.

Gently fold in the cooled almonds and extracts. Do not over mix.

Line 3 baking sheets with parchment paper and spray liberally with vegetable spray. Using a 1 ounce dipper or a large spoon, drop heaping tablespoons of the batter onto the baking sheets.

Cook at 250 degrees until lightly browned, about two hours. Turn the oven off and allow cookies to remain in the oven to cool for 1 1/2 to 2 hours.

Yield: 48 cookies

35 calories / 2.2 grams fat per cookie

APPLE CURRANT COBBLER

There are probably a million warm apple desserts out there, all of them good. Here's one more, lower in fat than most, with a dark, radiant garnet color.

4 cups apples, thinly sliced
1/2 cup red currant jelly
1 teaspoon lemon juice
1/2 cup whole wheat flour
1/2 cup brown sugar
1 teaspoon cinnamon
2 tablespoons corn oil margarine, cut into bits
1/2 cup pecans, chopped
Vegetable cooking spray

Thoroughly spray a deep 9-inch pie pan with vegetable spray. Layer in the apples.

Warm the jelly and lemon juice; pour over apples.

Mix the flour, sugar and cinnamon together; cut in bits of margarine until mixture is crumbly. Add the pecans. Top the mixture with apples and bake at 350 degrees for 30 minutes.

Serve warm with nonfat frozen vanilla yogurt.

Yield: 12 servings

110 calories / 2.5 grams fat per serving

PEACHES POACHED IN CHAMPAGNE

We like to make this one when Texas Hill Country peaches are at their peak; we use Texas champagne also.

2 cups dry champagne
1/2 cup sugar
1 vanilla bean, split, or 1 tablespoon vanilla extract
12 medium peaches, peeled and halved

Combine the champagne and sugar. Bring to a boil.

Scrape the seeds from the vanilla bean. Add the seeds and bean to the champagne.

Add the peach halves, cut side down, cover and simmer for five minutes. Turn the peaches and simmer, covered, for five more minutes.

Remove the peaches with a slotted spoon. Repeat the process until all the peach halves are cooked.

Bring the champagne mixture to a boil and reduce to 3/4 cup. Strain out the vanilla bean and pour the liquid over the peaches. Chill before serving.

Yield: 24 servings

88 calories / 1 gram fat per serving

PEARS IN CHIANTI

A romantic, classically European pairing of fruit and wine produce this deceptively simple, decidedly dramatic dinner party dessert. This colorful fruit and wine pairing makes a wonderful "do ahead" dinner party dessert.

4 cups Chianti
1 cup sugar
1/2 cup apple juice concentrate
1 teaspoon whole black peppercorns
2 bay leaves
2 two inch strips of lemon peel
1/4 cup lemon juice
8 pears, peeled, halved, cored

Bring all ingredients, except the pears, to a boil.

Place the pears in a pan just big enough to fit, pour the wine mix over and simmer until pears are tender, fifteen to thirty minutes.

Remove the pears and reduce the liquid until syrupy. Spoon over the pears and chill.

Yield: 16 servings

106 calories / .4 grams fat per serving

RASPBERRY-RHUBARB-PEAR COMPOTE

Rhubarb ...., is it a fruit or a vegetable? Actually, it's a vegetable, a member of the buckwheat family. Vegetables for dessert; you can't get any healthier than that.

6 ounces frozen raspberries, thawed
1/3 pound rhubarb or 7 ounces frozen rhubarb, trimmed and cut into 1" pieces
1 cup pears, peeled, cored and diced
1/2 cup sugar
3 tablespoons flour
Zest from 1 orange
1 teaspoon cinnamon
Vegetable cooking spray

Combine ingredients, bake in sprayed baking dish at 425 degrees for 30 minutes. Cool.

Spoon over vanilla frozen yogurt.

Yield: 6 servings

28 calories / .5 grams fat per serving

HONEY BAKED PEAR IN PHYLLO

This will be just the dessert if toga parties ever come back around. Try serving it after the Athenian chicken dish found in this book on page 185.

1 cup white wine
1/4 cup sugar
1 whole clove
1 one inch cinnamon stick
3 medium pears, peeled, halved and cored
1 1/2 teaspoons vanilla extract
2 ounces ricotta cheese
1 teaspoon marigold mint, chopped
1/4 cup honey
Phyllo pastry
Vegetable cooking spray

Combine wine, sugar, spices and poach pears until tender; about 15 minutes. Remove pears.

Add vanilla to liquid and reduce by half.

Stuff pear halves with ricotta cheese and Mexican marigold mint. Coat with honey. Wrap in phyllo, sealing the edges with honey. Spray with vegetable spray.

Bake at 375 degrees for 5-7 minutes or until golden. Serve on a pool of the wine and sugar reduction.

Yield: 6 servings

126 calories / 1.5 grams fat per serving

KEY LIME CHEESECAKE

The creamy lime filling and spicy gingersnap crust are a great combination. Use a little green food coloring if you want a more colorful lime pie.

12 gingersnaps
1 tablespoon low calorie margarine, softened
9 ounces tofu, sliced and drained between paper towels
1/2 cup low fat ricotta cheese
2 eggs and 1 egg white
1/2 cup evaporated skim milk
6 tablespoons flour
2 teaspoons baking powder
1/2 cup fresh squeezed lime juice
1 tablespoon lime zest
2/3 cup apple juice concentrate

Preheat the oven to 350 degrees. Crush the gingersnaps and combine with the margarine and cover the bottom of a 9 inch pie pan or spring form pan.

Combine the remaining ingredients in a food processor and blend thoroughly. Pour the mixture into the prepared pan and let sit for five minutes.

Bake until center appears firm, about thirty minutes.

Chill before slicing.

Yield: 16 servings

89 calories / 3.5 grams fat per serving

LEMONY CHEESE PIE WITH RASPBERRY SAUCE

Lemon with raspberry sauce is a great combination. OK, so just about anything with raspberry sauce is a great combination. For more about how to take advantage of this happy universal truth, look up the recipe for Raspberry Sauce on page 266.

16 ounces low fat cottage cheese
5 egg whites
3/4 cup evaporated skim milk
1 tablespoon nonfat dry milk powder
2/3 cup apple juice concentrate
3 tablespoons cornstarch
1/4 cup lemon zest
1 teaspoon vanilla
1/4 teaspoon cream of tartar
1 1/2 cup raisin bran cereal, crushed
1/4 cup sliced almonds
1 cup raspberry sauce (page 266)
Vegetable cooking spray

Preheat the oven to 325 degrees.

Puree the cottage cheese, 2 egg whites and 1/4 cup evaporated milk in a food processor until smooth. Add the remaining skim milk, dry milk, apple juice concentrate and blend again.

Add the cornstarch, lemon juice, zest and vanilla. Blend well.

In a separate bowl, beat the 3 remaining egg whites with the cream of tartar until stiff. Fold the beaten whites into the cheese mixture.

Spray a spring form pan with the spray and sprinkle the pan with the cereal mix. Pour in the prepared filling. Top with the almonds and bake for one hour at 325 degrees.

Turn off the oven and let the pie sit in the oven to cool for thirty minutes. Chill before slicing. Serve with the raspberry sauce.

Yield: 16 servings

118 calories / 1.5 grams fat per serving

SWEET POTATO PIE

Our version of this Southern favorite is as good for you as it is just plain good.

1 pound sweet potatoes
2 eggs
2 egg whites, beaten stiff
2/3 cup honey
1 2/3 cup evaporated skim milk
1 1/2 teaspoons cinnamon
1 teaspoon ginger
1/2 teaspoon ground cloves
12 gingersnaps, crushed
1 tablespoon margarine

Slice then steam the sweet potatoes until tender. Drain, peel, and press into a measuring cup to yield 1 1/2 cups.

Combine sweet potatoes with remaining ingredients, except the beaten egg whites, and process in a food processor or blender until smooth.

Fold in the beaten egg whites.

Make a crust of the gingersnaps and margarine and press into a 9 inch pie pan or springform pan. Pour in the prepared filling.

Bake the pie at 400 degrees for ten minutes. Lower the oven to 350 degrees and bake for 35 minutes or until center is set. Chill before slicing.

Yield: 16 servings

145 calories / 2.25 grams fat per serving

CHOCOLATE MOUSSE WITH GRAND MARNIER

After trying about a dozen different versions of chocolate mousse recipes, none of which seemed to fill the bill, once again we found that the ever versatile yogurt cheese provided the answer.

1/2 cup yogurt cheese (see glossary)
1 ounce dark sweet chocolate
4 egg whites
1/4 cup sugar
3 tablespoons cocoa powder
2 teaspoons grated orange zest
2 tablespoons Grand Marnier

Melt the chocolate in a double boiler and combine with yogurt cheese in a bowl.

Combine the egg whites and sugar in a stainless steel mixing bowl. Place the bowl over simmering water and whip the egg whites for 3 minutes. Remove from heat and continue to whip until soft peaks form.

Sift the cocoa twice and blend with the chocolate and yogurt mixture. Add the orange zest and Grand Marnier. Place this mixture over the simmering water and mix until warm and smooth.

Place the bowl of beaten egg whites over a larger bowl of ice water and fold the chocolate mixture in gently. Divide the mixture into parfait glasses and chill.

Yield: 6 servings

116 calories / 2.5 grams fat per serving

RASPBERRY MOUSSE

This recipe may be made with fresh raspberries or thawed frozen raspberries.

2 envelopes gelatin
1/2 cup orange juice
16 ounces raspberries
1 teaspoon orange zest
14 ounces well chilled evaporated skim milk
6 egg whites at room temperature
1 tablespoon lemon juice
1/8 teaspoon cream of tartar
1 teaspoon vanilla extract
1 tablespoon Kirsch (optional)
1 cup sugar free raspberry preserves

Dissolve the gelatin in the orange juice over low heat. Allow to cool.

Puree the raspberries and orange zest and set aside.

Freeze the milk, beaters and bowl until ice crystals begin to form around the edges of the bowl. (About twenty minutes.) Whip the evaporated milk to a whipped cream consistency.

Whip the egg whites to soft peaks. Add the lemon juice and cream of tartar and beat until stiff. Add the cooled orange juice and gelatin.

Fold the vanilla and Kirsch into the egg whites. Fold in the berry mixture and the preserves. Fold in the whipped milk. Spoon into mousse glasses and serve.

Yield: 8 servings

104 calories / .4 grams fat per one cup serving

PUMPKIN FLAN

Pity the poor pumpkin. Inexorably typecast (an unfortunate fate that also plagues the bird in this twin billing) as the inevitable denouement to Thanksgiving dinner, but capable of playing a much wider range of roles. For savory soups and side vegetables; for breads and cookies and cakes (and, in this case, a cool custard) let us also give thanks.

1-1/2 cups sugar (divided in half)
4 tablespoons water
2 eggs
2 egg whites
1/2 teaspoon vanilla extract
1/8 teaspoon nutmeg
1 3/4 cups 1% milk
1 1/2 cups pumpkin, cooked and mashed

Combine 3/4 cup sugar and water in saucepan. Caramelize to syrupy consistency over medium heat, stirring. Pour into eight custard cups, tipping cups to distribute syrup.

Combine remaining sugar, eggs, whites, vanilla, nutmeg and milk in bowl and beat with electric mixer until sugar dissolves. Add pumpkin and combine until smooth.

Pour into cups, place in water bath (large pan with one inch water); bake at 325 degrees for one and one-half hours or until knife inserted at center comes out clean. Cool out of water, then chill. Loosen edges, invert on a plate.

Yield: 8 servings

145 calories / 2 grams fat per serving

RASPBERRY CREME BRULEE

The French discover flan. A rose by any other name would be as sweet.

2 cups 2% milk
2 tablespoons nonfat dry milk powder
3/4 cup egg substitute
1/3 cup and 2 tablespoons sugar
1 teaspoon vanilla
30 raspberries

Blend milk and milk powder together. Add egg substitute, 1/3 of cup sugar and vanilla.

Place five raspberries in the bottom of 6 six-ounce custard cups. Pour mixture over and bake custard cups in a pan filled with one inch of water at 325 degrees for 35 minutes or until custard is set. Chill.

Sprinkle 1/2 teaspoon sugar over the top of each custard. Broil four inches from broiler until caramelized.

Yield: 6 servings

141 calories / 2 grams fat per serving

BITTERSWEET FUDGE SAUCE

If you are the sort of person who likes to go where others have not gone, to do what others have not done, then resist dipping your finger into this intensely dark and chocolate sauce before serving. You will, almost assuredly, be the first to do so.

1/3 cup unsweetened cocoa
1/3 cup packed brown sugar
1 tablespoon instant coffee
1 teaspoon cornstarch
2/3 cup evaporated skim milk
1/3 cup water

Combine the first four ingredients in a small sauce pan. Stir in the milk and water. Cook over medium heat until thickened.

Serve warm over frozen nonfat vanilla yogurt.

Yield: 1 1/2 cups

28 calories / .2 grams fat per tablespoon

RASPBERRY SAUCE

Raspberry sauce, like found money, goes well with just about everything! Try it (the berry, not the bucks) under anything chocolate, over frozen yogurt, as an accompaniment to lemon desserts, coupled with crepes, pooled with peaches, or paired with pears. You get the picture; and the picture is worth a thousand words, most of them laudatory.

Substitute fresh or frozen blackberries for a similar sauce that pairs especially well with our lemon roll.

2 cups fresh or thawed frozen raspberries
1 tablespoon powdered sugar
1 teaspoon cornstarch dissolved in 1 tablespoon water

Combine all ingredients in a small saucepan. Heat until bubbly. Strain through a mesh strainer, pushing out solids with the back of a spoon. Discard the seeds.

Chill and serve with chocolate torte, ice cream, or lemon cheesecake.

Yield: 1 cup

10 calories / .08 grams fat per tablespoon

RUM MANGO SAUCE

Just the stuff to blow you down and shiver your timbers after a tough day of plundering and pillaging down on the Spanish Main (or the local mall). If fresh mangoes are unavailable, try the bottled, available in most grocery stores now.

1 3/4 cups peeled, cubed mango
2/3 cup evaporated skim milk
1/4 cup light rum
2 tablespoons brown sugar
1 1/2 teaspoons lime juice
Extra mango cubes for garnish

Puree the first five ingredients in a food processor or blender until smooth.

Serve over vanilla frozen yogurt, or a warm spice cake.

Yield: 3 cups

32 calories / .6 grams fat per tablespoon

SWEET CHERRY SAUCE WITH GRAND MARNIER

Share in a chef's secret: it's the sauce that sets the dish apart. A splash of color and fruit, fortified with a little liqueur will elevate the simplest of desserts to three star status.

1/3 cup sugar
1 tablespoon cornstarch
1/8 teaspoon salt
1/4 cup water
1 teaspoon lemon juice
1 pound pitted cherries, fresh or unsweetened frozen, thawed
3 tablespoons Grand Marnier
1/2 teaspoon orange zest

Whisk all ingredients together in a small saucepan. Cook over medium heat, stirring constantly until slightly thickened. Chill.

Serve over ice cream or frozen yogurt, or cheesecake.

Yield: 3 cups

22 calories / .1 grams fat per tablespoon

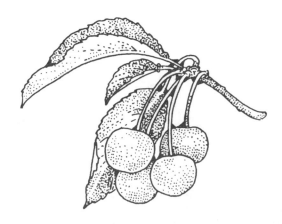

MUD PIE

Who named this thing, anyway? Well, no matter, you can be sure when you serve it that everyone will have "mud on their faces" in short order, and be glad for it.

1 1/2 cups cinnamon snaps, crushed
1 tablespoon margarine, melted
1 quart coffee frozen yogurt
6 ounces Bittersweet Fudge Sauce (page 265)
1/4 cup slivered almonds, toasted

Make a crust with cookies and margarine. Press into a nine inch pie tin.

Fill with yogurt. Freeze hard. Top with Fudge Sauce and almonds.

Yield: 12 servings

132 calories / 2.25 grams fat per serving

SICILIAN LEMON ORANGE SHERBET

This light, bright and perfectly refreshing dessert takes several hours to freeze properly, so allow plenty of time.

1 tablespoon julienned orange peel
1 tablespoon julienned lemon peel
1 cup water
1/3 cup powdered sugar
1 1/4 cups orange juice
3/4 cup tangerine juice
1/2 cup lemon juice

Pare just the outer skin from the fruit, using a vegetable parer and cut into fine slivers. Combine with the water and sugar in a small saucepan. Bring to a simmer, stirring to dissolve the sugar. Cook until the liquid is reduced to 3/4 cup. Strain the julienne from the liquid and set aside.

Add the sugar syrup to the juices and freeze in a large metal bowl. Whisk the mixture thoroughly about every half hour until it has achieved a sherbet-like consistency.

Serve in chilled cups and garnish with an orange slice and a little of the reserved sugared peel.

Yield: 4 servings

75 calories / .2 grams fat per one cup serving

STRAWBERRY SHERBET

Although you will need to plan ahead for this one, the actual preparation time is only about five minutes. If the mixture should freeze solid, (if left overnight) simply set out to thaw slightly and re-whip.

3/4 cup water
1/4 cup sugar
12 ounce can of strawberry nectar
6 cups unsweetened frozen strawberries, slightly thawed
Juice of one lemon

Dissolve the sugar in the water in a small saucepan over medium heat. Add to a food processor along with the other ingredients and puree until smooth.

Place the mixture in a large metal mixing bowl and freeze, whisking briefly and scraping down the sides of the bowl, about every 45 minutes until the mixture is firm. (About 3 to 4 hours.)

Yield: 8 cups

75 calories / 0 grams fat per 1/2 cup serving

SAMPLE MENUS AND NUTRIENT ANALYSIS

LASR SAMPLE MENU
DAY 1

BREAKFAST

     1 Cup Nonfat Milk

     1 Cup Orange Juice

     Blueberry Blue Corn Fritters with Chile Honey
(page 50)

MORNING SNACK

     Orange

LUNCH

     Squash Torte with Salsa Verde (page 162)

     Mixed Carrots, Green Beans and Browned Onion
Slices

AFTERNOON SNACK

     3 Dates

APPETIZER

     Crab Quesadillas (page 214)

DINNER

     3 Oz. Smoked Pork Tenderloin with Blackberry Sauce
(page 176)

     Succotash

     Orange Glazed Butternut Squash

     Salad (Lettuce, Carrots, Red Pepper, Sprouts, Tomato,
Cucumbers, Fat Free Dressing)

     Pumpkin Flan (page 263)

EVENING SNACK

     3 Cups Air Popped Corn

	Exchange	Actual
MILK		1.0
VEG		6.0
FRUIT		3.5
BREAD		4.9
MEAT		3.3
FAT		2.5

LASR SAMPLE MENU
DAY 2

BREAKFAST

       1 Cup Nonfat Milk

       Asparagus Frittata (from Spa Specialties)

MORNING SNACK

       Plum

LUNCH

       Lentil Soup with Chile and Lime (page 106)

       Spinach Filled Corn Crepes with a Smoked Tomato Sauce (page 149)

       Orange Glazed Carrots

AFTERNOON SNACK

       Apple

APPETIZER

       Smoked Trout Spread with Horseradish Cream on Rice Crackers (page 184)

DINNER

       Chicken in Raspberry Vinegar (page 196)

       Broccoli with Mock Hollandaise (page 70)

       White Bean Gratinee (page 144)

       Salad (Lettuce, Carrots, Sprouts, Tomato, Cucumbers, Fat Free Dressing)

       Frozen Coffee Torte (page 269) with Warm Fudge Sauce (page 265)

EVENING SNACK

       3 Cups Air Popped Corn

	Exchange	Actual
MILK		1.4
VEG		8.0
FRUIT		2.0
BREAD		4.2
MEAT		2.5
FAT		3.2

LASR SAMPLE MENU
DAY 3

BREAKFAST

    1 Cup Nonfat Milk
    Gingerbread Pancakes (page 52) with 1/4 Cup Pureed
    Blueberries

LUNCH

    Split Pea Soup
    Smoked Turkey Reuben Sandwich (page 206)
    1/2 Cup Cooked Fresh Asparagus

AFTERNOON SNACK

    Banana

APPETIZER

    Artichoke Puffs (from Spa Specialties)

DINNER

    Salmon Croquettes (page 219)
    Honey Glazed Acorn Squash
    Wild Brown Rice with Mushrooms
    Salad (Lettuce, Carrots, Sprouts, Tomato, Cucumbers, Fat
    Free Dressing)
    Blueberry Spice Cake (page 236)

EVENING SNACK

    3 Cups Air Popped Corn

Exchange	ActuaL
MILK	0.9
VEG	5.3
FRUIT	2.3
BREAD	7.9
MEAT	5.8
FAT	0.9

GLOSSARY

GLOSSARY OF INGREDIENTS

ADOBO

Spanish for "sauce or dressing". Not to be confused with <u>adobe</u>, the dried earthen building block (a mistake which, if made, will cause unpredictable but generally unsatisfactory results in most recipes). Adobos usually consist of tomatoes, onions, chiles, and seasonings stewed together, then used to season other foods. Canned chipotle chiles are often packed in adobo.

BUCKWHEAT

Actually a small, seed-like fruit rather than a true grain. Not to be confused with a character actor of the same name from the "Our Gang" days (see caution above). Whole, used similarly to rice as a side dish known as "kasha"; or ground into flour, to make muffins and pancakes.

CARABEEF

Trade name for the meat from hormone and antibiotic free water buffalo which are raised on a ranch in Arkansas. Ounce for ounce it has less fat than boneless, skinless chicken breast and it cooks, looks, and tastes just like extremely lean beef, which is exactly what it is. It comes in just about all the cuts you are familiar with, (including a great, ultra lean sausage!) and it is a big hit at our weekend barbecues at the resort. If you would like to know how to get some of this good stuff for yourself, give the fine folks at Carabeef a holler; they will ship to you direct or provide you the name of a retail source in your area. Phone them at 1-800-264-7481, or write: Carabeef, P.O. Box 1094, Lake Charles, Louisiana 70602.

CHILES

Commonly known as 'peppers' or 'chili peppers' to most of us. Their cultivation as a food source pre-dates the Aztecs. A note of caution, chiles get their 'heat' from an irritatingly adhesive substance called 'capsaicin' that inevitably clings to your skin when you handle them. Be sure to wash thoroughly with soap and water after preparation. You can temper the heat in any chile by seeding it and using only the flesh part. A list of the more common favorites follows; most of them are available in better grocery stores.

ANAHEIM: Elongated, pale to bright green, ripening to red, usable in all stages. Slightly to medium hot, an excellent choice for green chile sauces and for stuffing.

ANCHO: A dried poblano chile. Dark mahogany color, wrinkled, about the size and shape of the palm of your hand. The best ones are still slightly pliable and have a rich, prune-like aroma. Used in cooked sauces. Medium hot to hot.

CHIPOTLE: A smoked jalapeno chile. Available dried or more commonly, canned in adobo sauce. Very hot, with a delicious barbecued flavor.

HABAÑERO: The world's hottest chile. Considered inedibly incendiary by some, revered by others. Small, bright orange, lantern shaped fruit. Rarely seen fresh; more commonly bottled in 'tabasco' style sauces.

JALAPEÑO: Thumb-sized, bright to dark green, hot. Try thin, seeded slivers of the fresh rather than the pickled version that makes a nacho macho.

POBLANO: The traditional stuffing chile in Mexico. Dark green, slightly hot to hot.

SERRANO: Small, elongated, bright green, hot. Similar in use and flavor to the jalapeno.

CILANTRO

A pungently aromatic leafy green herb used extensively in Mexican and Thai cookery. Also known as Chinese parsley. If fresh is unavailable, omit rather than substitute.

CRABMEAT

When called for in this book, fresh Gulf Coast lump blue crabmeat is intended. Other types of fresh or frozen crabmeat may be substituted; but avoid the canned and imitation varieties which are tasteless and high in sodium.

EXTRA VIRGIN OLIVE OIL

Designates oil from the very first pressing of the olives, an indication of quality. Different brands can be as varied in color, aroma and flavor as wines. Experiment to find your favorites.

JICAMA

A grapefruit sized tuber generally peeled and eaten raw in salads. Has a potato-apple like crunch and flavor. Often consumed simply diced and sprinkled with lime juice and chili powder.

MARGARINE

Use only margarines with a liquid oil listed as their first ingredient. By law, ingredients must be listed in order of predominance, and this insures a more healthy, highly polyunsaturated product.

MASA HARINA

The corn flour commonly used for making tortillas, tamales, and the like. Available in the flour section of your favorite grocery store. (Quaker Oaks Co. distributes nationally).

PARMESAN CHEESE

One good rule of thumb, as regards its purchase: eschew such cheeses as are contained in cardboard canisters. That is to say, do not chew them. Or purchase them. Instead, head for the refrigerated deli section or, better yet, a cheese shop for the good stuff. It should have a heavy, moist feel when rolled between your thumb and forefinger and melt, almost immediately, on your tongue with deep, creamy, complex flavors.

PHYLLO PASTRY

Stacked sheets of newspaper-thin pastry dough, commonly associated with Greek cookery, but with a whole world of applications. Usually found in the frozen foods pastry section of your grocery store. Allow yourself a little time, and room to work with your first 'folding'; before long you'll be "wrapping" faster than an L.A. street musician.

PINE NUTS

The corn kernel shaped seed of the pinon tree. Prized for the delicate rich flavor, often enhanced by toasting, that it brings to a variety of savory sauces and foods. Blanched, sliced almonds may be substituted.

ROLLED OATS

Simply uncooked oats as commonly used to make oatmeal. Mares eat 'em. Does eat 'em. Little lambs prefer ivy.

ROUX

A cooked combination of fat and flour commonly used to thicken soups, sauces, etc. Pronounced "roo" as in kangaroo. Obviously has limited uses (as do kangaroos for that matter) in low fat cookery but in some instances is indispensable. See instruction in 'Cooking Techniques' for darkening.

TOMATILLO

A member of the gooseberry family that looks like, <u>but is not</u>, a small green tomato, a confusion compounded by its name. Used in a variety of Mexican salsas and soups. Available fresh in your produce department or perhaps canned at a specialty foods store.

VINEGAR

Good vinegar should cascade across your palate in a pleasant rush of acid and fruit, not simply assault your tastebuds with sour. As much care should be taken in its selection as a wine for your table. Most of the vinegars we use are distilled from wine (although a good cider vinegar has its place) and can be broken down into three basic categories: <u>Balsamic</u> - an Italian wine vinegar, aged in wooden casks and prized for its mellow, rounded flavor. <u>Herbal</u> - we make, use and market an extensive selection, steeping fresh herbs from our organic gardens in good red and white wine vinegar stock. Some of our favorite combinations are cilantro and garlic or basil with garlic chives in red wine vinegar and rosemary with garlic, jalapenos and black peppercorn and our lemon vinegar with five different lemon flavored herbs. <u>Fruit</u> - we also produce a selection of fruited vinegars utilizing raspberries, blueberries and the like which we use in sauces and salad dressings.

YOGURT CHEESE

You won't find it in any store, it's the cheese you make with the yogurt cheese funnel. (An order form for the funnel is included in the back of the book.) Use yogurt that does <u>not</u> contain gelatin or stabilizers or it won't separate to make the cheese. Simply place the yogurt in the funnel, place over a glass or jar to drain and leave for 12 to 48 hours. The longer it drains, the thicker it will be. It may be refrigerated or allowed to drain outside the refrigerator. After the liquid part of the yogurt, the whey, has drained it may be discarded and you are left with yogurt cheese. If you start with nonfat yogurt, your yogurt cheese will be nonfat also. The cheese then can be used for everything from dips to desserts or to replace sour cream and cream cheese in recipes. When cooking with yogurt cheese, you will need to stabilize it with one tablespoon of cornstarch per cup of cheese or 2 egg whites or 1 egg. A good source of calcium and protein.

ZEST

The finely grated rind of any citrus fruit. It imparts to many dishes the very quality for which it was no doubt named.

II.   COOKING TERMS AND TECHNIQUES

BLANCHING

The brief (usually for only 30 seconds or so) introduction of food into a large pot of rapidly boiling water. This is helpful in loosening the skins of some vegetables and soft fruits, facilitating their removal; or in the preparation of some leafy vegetables that require very, very little cooking.

BUTTERFLY

To make a horizontal incision almost, but not quite, all the way through a piece of meat or seafood for the purpose of opening it for stuffing or spreading it thinner for more rapid cooking, a process which, curiously enough, is seldom applied to butterflies.

CARAMELIZED SUGAR

Place an amount of granulated sugar in a heavy skillet and, stirring constantly with a wooden spoon, cook over medium heat until darkened. Stir in an equal amount of liquid (usually but not always, water), carefully. This caramel syrup is used in desserts and some sauces. Onions or other vegetables that have been sauteed until they release their natural sugars and turn brown are also said to have been "caramelized".

CHARRING

For our purposes, this is the process of blackening and blistering the skin of a vegetable over open flame. This is sometimes done to facilitate removal of the outer layer (see 'roasting peppers') or sometimes to create a particular flavor or character as in charred tomato sauces, where the blackened skin is incorporated into the dish.

CLARIFIED BUTTER OR MARGARINE

Melt one stick in a small saucepan over medium heat; continue cooking until it stops sputtering. Set aside, then skim and discard the thin crust of salts that will form on the surface. Carefully pour the liquified fat into another container leaving behind the solid residue on the bottom. This liquid is now 'clarified'. It has a much higher 'burn' temperature than the unclarified equivalent and may be used successfully in small amounts for sauteed dishes. Please note that 'dietetic' margarines simply have more air and water incorporated into them and if clarified will contain amounts of fat, teaspoon for teaspoon, equal to their 'regular' counterpart.

DEGLAZING

The process of scraping up the crusted food particles left behind in a roasting pan or skillet in which a piece of meat has been cooked. Use a wooden spoon and some liquid (usually stock, wine or vinegar), scraping vigorously to loosen every bit. The resulting enriched liquid is then typically incorporated into a sauce for the meat.

ROASTING CHILES

All chiles (or peppers) are sheathed in a thin translucent exterior skin that gives them their shiny appearance. When eaten raw, this skin is of little detriment, but cooked it begins to separate from the flesh of the chile, displaying all of the aesthetic appeal and nutritional value of that substance it most closely resembles: cellophane. Consequently it is generally removed, by roasting the pepper over an open flame, for recipes requiring a cooked chile. This may be accomplished by using an indoor or outdoor grill, a stove top gas burner, or even an oven broiler, but in all cases the object is the same: to blacken and blister the exterior of the chile. Plunge the thoroughly charred chile into cold water, then gently peel away the blackened portion. Make a lengthwise slit in the chile, open it slightly and remove the clump of seeds at the stem end. Your chile is now ready for stuffing, or sauces.

ROUX

Because of its inherent fat content, roux plays a very limited role as a thickening agent in any lean leaning cuisine. Additional pureed vegetables or a cornstarch slurry suffice handsomely in most cases as a non fat alternative. The most notable exception to this being Cajun cookery where darkened rouxs are essential to the authenticity and vigor of the finished dish. The saving grace here, in our recipes, is that very little additional fat is introduced into the dishes, and the resulting fat content, in context of the finished product, comes in at very acceptable levels. Darkening a roux properly, without burning it, may take anywhere from 20 to 30 minutes during which time your participation must remain constant, your devotion absolute. You will want a heavy skillet (we like cast iron) proportionate in size to the amount of roux being darkened - the roux should just cover the bottom in a thin layer. Using a whisk or wooden spoon, stir this mixture steadily, without stopping, over medium low to low heat until the roux reaches the desired color. It should deepen from blond to honey to chestnut to oxblood to finally a black almost purple with a sheen you can see your reflection in. At this point, stir in the diced vegetables (have them cut and close at hand) almost always called for (this helps to cool the mixture down), mix all thoroughly together, turn off the heat and continue to stir for a couple of minutes. Proceed as the recipe indicates.

SAUTE

Traditionally this means cooking food over high heat in a skillet with a moderate amount of fat. Here are some tips that will give you means of reaching the same end using less fat. Use a heavy skillet with a non stick surface. Be sure the skillet is hot before introducing the food. Spray the surface of the skillet lightly with a non stick vegetable spray. Pat the food surfaces dry, then spray lightly with the same spray. Use thinly cut pieces of meat or vegetables so that they can cook through without burning. Use medium to medium high temperatures: you want enough to seal the exterior surfaces and brown them but not so much as to burn - adjust. Don't overcook (approximately 10 minutes per inch of total thickness will be enough-if in doubt, cut a small slit into the piece and peek!). If you are sauteing breaded foods, the addition of just a little clarified margarine (see Glossary I), about 1/3 teaspoon per serving, will greatly enhance the final result with about a gram of fat per serving increase.

STOCKS

Constructing a stew, a soup or a sauce from water is, for many of us, the culinary equivalent of kissing your sister. Canned stocks, now available with more reasonable sodium levels, are not the very best answer, but, especially if simmered briefly with a few vegetables, a superior alternative (an elevation, at least, to kissing cousins). The best stocks, however, the ones you make yourself from scratch, imbue the dishes in which they are used with depth, dimension, and character. Even passion. Admirable qualities in too short supply all around these days. So we encourage you to take stock, and make same. Here's a recipe(s) to get you started:

Our Stock Stock Recipe

1 rainy Sunday afternoon
1 large pot
Some vegetables: an onion or two, a couple or three carrots, same for celery ribs, all chopped into large, comfortably sized pieces, along with as many garlic cloves as you deem prudent (at least one, probably no more than six). Now these are the basics; you may wish to add, particularly if you are making a strictly vegetable stock, more of all of the above plus a few green beans, tomatoes, parsnips, a turnip, some spinach or other greens, etc.
Some herbs: Several parsley stems, a couple of bay leaves, a dozen or so whole black peppercorns, at least a half teaspoon or more of leaf thyme, rosemary, oregano, marjoram - any or all (if you are using fresh herbs, double the amount)
Some bones and meat: You can make stock with either/or but the best (with an emphasis on bones) requires both. You will want 4 to 5 pounds total.
Beef: Your meat market usually sells inexpensive soup bones; choose any lean, cheap cut for meat. As preparation for the stock, roast the bones, along with the cubed meat, and some of the carrots and onions in a pan

at 425 degrees for 45 minutes or so, turning occasionally. Add to the pot, de-glaze (see Glossary I) the pan and proceed.

<u>Chicken:</u> Two whole birds or enough parts to equal, plus any additional available bones (if you are the sort of person who saves and freezes the carcasses of roasted chickens for just such a occasion, bless you).

<u>Seafood:</u> If your seafood market filets whole fish, they will probably, with some notice, save and give you fish frames (skeletons). Shrimp and lobster shells, and oyster pot likker are other good flavor sources.

Some water: Enough to cover everything comfortably, a little more if you're not going to be checking in regularly; remember, though, you can always add more water and we want a stock that makes a statement, not an insinuation.

Some salt: Unless prohibited for health reasons a wee bit of salt rounds out the flavor of all stocks. You may want to consider the addition of a high quality bouillon cube (one per gallon) to provide salt and intensify flavor. Let your conscience be your guide.

Place your version of "everything" into the pot, bring to a boil, lower to a bare simmer, skimming the top of any scum that appears. Simmer for at least two hours, up to four hours. You may add more water as needed. Strain everything through a colander, pressing out the solids with the back of a large spoon to get every bit of goodness. Strain again through a finer sieve, then refrigerate overnight. All fat will rise to the top and solidify, facilitating its removal. Underneath you should find the gelatinous stock. Taste for strength, and further reduce on the stove, if necessary, to achieve the desired intensity. Use or freeze in conveniently sized containers until needed.

We leave you with this recipe, which is not so much a recipe as it is an idea, reminding that good beginnings often make for the very best endings.

COME′ CON GUSTO!

INDEX

Raspberry Creme Brulee 264
Raspberry Mousse 262
Raspberry Rhubarb Pear Compote
    256
Raspberry Sauce 266
Red Bean and Sausage Soup 97
Red Bean Chili 160
Red Chile Tartar Sauce 79
Relish 33, 66, 79
Rhubarb 256
Rice 64, 66, 108, 130, 148, 166,
    167, 176, 187,
    192, 220, 221,
    223, 233, 234,
    275, 277, 280
    Seafood Dirty Rice 220
    Vegetable Paella 166
Roasted Lemon Garlic Sauce 78
Roasted Red Pepper Sauce 80
Roasting peppers 102, 105, 227,
    286
Rum Mango Sauce 267
Salad dressings 115, 117, 284
Salads
    Pasta Salad 129
    Shrimp, Mango and Rice
        Salad 130
    Smoked Chicken Salad
        128
    Smoked Trout and Pasta
        131
    Tortellini with Salmon
        Salad 132
Salmon 54, 83, 98, 132, 210,
    217, 219, 277
    Blackened Salmon 210
    Potato Wrapped Salmon
        217
    Salmon Potato Croquettes
        219
    Tortellini with Salmon
        Salad 132
Salmon Potato Croquettes 219
Salsa Picante 81
Salsa Verde 77
Salsas 59, 75, 81, 147, 181, 214,
    284
    Chipotle Papaya Relish
        66
    Chipotle Salsa 69

Mango Salsa 75
Pico de Gallo 76
Salsa Picante 81
Salsa Verde 77
San Antonio Bay Crabcakes 224
Sandwiches 124
    Meatless Muffeletta 159
    Smoked Turkey Reubens
        206
Sauces 26, 54, 59, 65, 70, 81,
    134, 156, 162,
    181, 281, 283,
    284, 286, 287
    Basil Cream Sauce 60
    Bittersweet Fudge Sauce
        265
    Black Bean Sauce 199
    Black Magic Barbecue
        Sauce 63
    Blackberry Sauce 176
    Cajun Demiglace 61
    Chipotle Mayonnaise 65
    Creole Mustard Sauce
        201
    Green Chile Sauce 67
    Hollandaise Variations
        71
    Honey Lime Garlic Glaze
        73
    Horseradish Cream 184
    Lime Mustard Sauce 74
    Lime, Garlic and Leek
        Sauce 217
    Mango Sauce 198
    Mock Hollandaise 70
    Mock Sour Cream 72
    Orange Ginger Sauce
        241
    Pepper Sauce (Spanish
        Potato Torte)
        164
    Raspberry Sauce 266
    Red Chile Tartar Sauce
        79
    Red Pepper Sauce 226
    Roasted Lemon Garlic
        Sauce 78
    Roasted Red Pepper
        Sauce 80
    Rum Mango Sauce 267

Lake Austin Spa Resort

1705 S. Quinlan Park Road
Austin, TX 78732
1-800-847-5637
www.lakeaustin.com
e-mail: info@lakeaustin.com

Please send me the following (check the appropriate line):

___ copies of Lean Star Cuisine—*a great gift idea for bridal showers, house warmings, new home owners, birthdays, holidays, thank you's. . . you name it!*

___ information about Lake Austin Spa Resort's *next* healthy cookbook

___ additional information about the programs, packages, and spa treatments that Lake Austin Spa Resort offers day and overnight guests

Name:_____

Street Address:_____

City:_____State:_____Zip:_____

Home Phone:(_____)_____Work:(_____)_____

Form of Payment for Cookbook
_____Check _____Money Order _____VISA _____MC _____AMEX

Credit Card #:_____Exp. Date:_____

Signature:_____

Cost of Cookbook(s) $19.95 each   _____

7.25% tax if Texas resident   _____

Shipping $3.00 per book   _____

Total Amount Enclosed   _____

Call us about volume discounts or merchandising opportunities!